Research Methodology
in
EDUCATION

(Strictly on the basis of prescribed syllabus with modern trends)

Research Methodology in EDUCATION

(Strictly on the basis of prescribed syllabus with modern trends)

V K Shastri

AUTHORSPRESS

Worldwide Circulation through Authorspress Global Network
First Published 2008
by
Authorspress
E-35/103, Jawahar Park
Laxmi Nagar, Delhi-110 092
e-mail: authorspress@yahoo.com

Research Methodology in Education
ISBN 978-81-7273-461-9

Printed in India at Virgo Press, Delhi.

Preface

Major advances in educational research in the 20th century ensured that the knowledge imparted to students in the formal schooling set-up catered to the society's continually changing social, economic, political and cultural needs and concerns. As such, in a world where change is the only constant, educational research has become crucial to impart to students a broad spectrum of information and knowledge which can equip them with the necessary skills to carve their own niche in life. Educational research is not only necessary to brush up the schooling experience of students, but also assess the manner in which educational policies, trends and goals evolve.

The present text is an attempt to introduce the readers to the rigours and procedures of educational research, considering the import that it carries within the educational set-up. The emphasis is upon delineating the types of educational research, the processes involved in their implementation, and what they entail. Attention has been devoted to an understanding of the ways in which educational research itself has evolved, with a focus on current trends in the field aiding in highlighting this. In addition, the relevance of educational research has been continually underlined by the various critical perspectives included in each of the chapters, which seek to foster a better comprehension of educational research.

I firmly believe that the relevant and insightful content of the book will be of immense use and fill in the gapes between theory and practice to research scholars of education.

V K Shastri

Contents

1

Foundation of Educational Research

The term "research" is a combination of two words "Re" and "Search". "Re" means again and again, and "Search" refers to explore something new. Hence, research is a process of observing the phenomenon (i.e. any event, anything, any process etc) again and again, collecting the data and drawing some scientific conclusion on the basis of those data. In simple words, research refers to a search for knowledge.

Educational research is a systematic attempt to gain a better understanding of the educational process taking place inside or outside the classroom, generally with an aim of improving its efficiency. It represents an activity directed towards the development of an organised body of scientific knowledge about the events with which educators are concerned. Of central importance are the behaviour patterns of pupils, and particularly those to be learned through the educational process. A scientific body of knowledge about education should enable the educators to determine just what teaching and other learning conditions provide in order to produce desired aspects of learned behaviour among young people who attend school.

The main objective of educational research is to understand, explain, and to some extent predict and control human behaviour in educational settings. It is a process of development of organised and useful body of scientific knowledge, which the academicians are concerned with. It attempts to attain knowledge about the nature of children, how they learn and how they grow. It also tries to gather facts about the child's personality, learning process, emotional development, social adjustment and skills. It tries to study child's stages of growth and development and the factors influencing these with an aim to improving teaching-learning process in the classroom.

1.1. Characteristics of Educational Research

Educational research has largely applied the scientific method to the study of educational and/or classroom problems. It stresses the search for truth. It follows the scientific rules and procedures of research. The scientific method is based on certain basic postulates:

1. It relies only on empirical evidence, not on common sense.
2. It utilises relevant and related concepts only.
3. It is committed to only objective and unbiased considerations.
4. It makes only relevant, adequate and accurate statements.
5. It respects and responds to verification.
6. It leads to probabilistic predictions about the researched phenomena.
7. It aims at formulating scientific theories.

The scientific method encourages a rigorous, impersonal mode of procedure dictated by the demands of logic and objective procedure. This is an objective, logical and systematic method which is free from personal biases and prejudices. The nature of scientific method can be traced to the following:

i) *Logical and objective:* Educational research is logical and objective in nature, like other disciplines of science. It doesn't rely on subjective and illogical interpretation of the phenomena since these may not be true and scientific.

ii) *Systematic and accurate:* Educational research is nothing but systematic and accurate investigation of the educational problems in which data are collected and analysed as accurately as possible.

iii) *Generalisations:* Educational research gives due importance to the discovery of scientific principles and generalisations on the basis of which a wide range of problems may be solved.

iv) *Reliability and validity:* Educational research leads to, since it uses the scientific method, reliable findings that are collected only through the validated procedures. Its findings are dependable.

v) *Collection of primary data:* Educational research emphasises on the collection of the data from the primary or from the first hand sources, and it does not believe in what others say.

vi) *Purposive:* Educational research is purposive since it is led by the definite purpose of solving a particular problem.

vii) *Inter-disciplinary:* Educational research is inter-disciplinary, and an educational problem can be studied by several distinct disciplines such as psychology, sociology, economics, history, anthropology, etc.

viii) *Predictions:* Like the scientific method that possesses the ability and power of prediction, educational research also makes predictions about various educational phenomena.

ix) *Not as exact as research in physical sciences:* Educational research is a field of research of behaviour in educational settings and behaviour is a very complex phenomenon, which is always changing. Even an individual can behave differently in a similar situation next time. So, it cannot be as exact as are the research studies in the physical sciences.

x) *Not the field of an academician only:* Educational research is not the field of only that person who is exclusively and specifically trained in the field of education; rather, any sensitive researcher with a background in education can do research on any educational problem.

xi) *Not a costly affair:* Most of the educational and/or classroom research is not a costly affair. We generally don't need sophisticated labs, or instruments, rather what we need are inexpensive educational tests and tools, paper and pencil, library facilities, research publication facilities and subjects (i.e. students or teachers whose educational problems are to be studied and solved).

In a nutshell, on the basis of the above discussion it can be concluded that educational and/or classroom research is a science as well as an art, and its nature is scientific. All the characteristics of science are possessed by educational research. But doing research is not merely a science but an art also, because research is not a mechanical process; rather it requires the in-depth understanding of the problem to be studied, complete knowledge of the research process, and an insight into the skillful solution of research problems.

1.2. A Scientific and Disciplined Inquiry Approach

Educational research utilises sets of methods to provide trustworthy information about educational problems/issues. Research helps to provide "facts"/reliable information or verifiable information instead of assumptions.

A scientific and disciplined inquiry approach is based on systematic approach to examining educational issues and questions. It combines features of inductive and deductive reasoning with other characteristics to produce an approach to understanding that, though fallible, is generally more viable and reliable than traditions, experts, personal beliefs/experiences or inductive/deductive reasoning alone.

Research is always influenced by the researcher's subjectivity even though researchers try to be objective. The complexity of humans and the contexts within which research is contacted makes objectivity an impossible task. Attempts to follow a scientific inquiry requires the researcher to describe in detail the procedures used to conduct the research study-provides a basis for examination and verification of claims/the result. These checks and balances allows research studies to be critiqued in ways that are not available to critique traditions, personal experiences etc.

The following are the basic steps of a scientific inquiry

i) Recognise and identify a topic to be studied. A topic is a question, issue or problem related to education that can be examined and answered through the collection and analysis of data.

ii) Describe and execute the procedures to collect information about the topic being studied. This involves identify the subjects/participants, the measures needed to collect the data, and the activities describing how and when the data will be collected.

iii) Analyse the data.

iv) State the results or implications based on analysis of data. Conclusions reached in the research study should relate back to the original research topic.

1.3. Objectives of Educational Research

Research in education or classroom research is very inevitable for providing useful and dependable knowledge through which the process of education can be made more effective and its various purposes can be fulfilled. The various purposes of educational research are as follows, which show the need for research in education:

i) *Progress:* The ultimate aim of all research is progress. If God would had not gifted us with the talent of research, instead of living in houses we would still be living on the trees; instead of travelling by trains, and buses, we would be crossing miles on foot; instead of sending messages by e-mail through the internet and post office, we would still be using pigeons. It is only education and our ability to use language that has made our lives easier to live. And, improvement in anything is just impossible without the review of the situation or without research. If a person, a section or a nation is to grow, for which quality education is a must. To attain this goal, every nation continuously keeps a sharp eye on its present educational standard, its limitations and shortcomings, and on the scope of improvement for quality education. And this is possible only through educational research. So, educational research leads to better quality of life of a human being and the progress of a nation.

ii) *System:* Education is not just a means of educating a person but aims at his/her overall personality development. Quality and systematic education can only attain this aim. Educational research aims at developing such a system. Specifying the importance of research, J. W. Best writes, "research is considered to be more formal, systematic, intensive process of carrying on the scientific method of analysis. It involves a more systematic structure of investigation, usually resulting in some sort of formal record of procedures and a report of results or conclusions."

iii) *Economy:* Decisions can both be taken as either thoughtfully or thoughtlessly. Naturally, thoughtless decisions mislead, and lead only to failure or frustration. But thoughtful decisions, taken on some solid ground, e.g., on the basis of some systematic research, save time, money, energy and a lot of failure and frustration. This economy leads us to progress. Educational research guides us and shows us the adequate and accurate path that how should we take next step toward success, quality educational, quality life, and progress of the nation. If we take steps blindfolded we cannot move far.

iv) *Theory building:* A discipline can be considered rich on the basis of the scientific theories it has. While education is a discipline by itself, it has derived from disciplines like philosophy, psychology, sociology, history, etc. These disciplines have considerable effect on the field of education, and there is a great need to build sound and scientific theories so that the advantage of its interaction with other disciplines can be taken. This will result in broadening the scope of education and utilising this interactive knowledge in the field of education. And, it is possible through educational research.

v) *Discipline development:* Education is both a science and an art. As a science, it has a vast treasure of knowledge about the nature of human learning and mind, its growth and development, effective strategies of imparting education, programmes and practices adopted by different countries, etc. There is still a great need to add scientific knowledge to it in order to explore the unexplored. As an art, education aims at imparting the knowledge to the pupils effectively.

vi) *Expansion of education:* The field of education is continuously expanding which has resulted in various types of problems. Solving these problems just on the basis of see or trial and error can be very harmful. So, we are in a great need of educational research that will provide us with scientific solutions to various educational problems.

vii) *Changing concept of education:* As a result of the rapid scientific and technological changes, a great need is also felt to change the old fashioned curriculum, textbooks, methods of teaching and evaluation, etc. Improvements in these can only be introduced after conducting careful educational research. Social and vocational needs are also rapidly changing. Hence, in the present age, vocationalisation of education is being given top priority. So, educational research is a must that can suggest appropriate and effective changes as per the need of current scientific era.

1.4. Areas of Educational Research

Major areas of educational research are:

— Pre-primary education

— Primary education

— Secondary Education

— Higher Education

— Agricultural and technical education

— Non-formal education

— Teaching process

Pre-Primary Education: Pre-primary education is highly essential for the physical, emotional and intellectual growth of the children because some research studies have revealed that children who attended pre-primary schools showed better progress at the primary level. So, public and private sectors and agencies must explore ways and means to promote pre-primary education.

Primary Education: In Article 45 of the Indian Constitution, the Directive Principle provides for free and compulsory education for all children in the age range of 6-14 years, but this objective has not been fully achieved. So, research is required to find out the possible causes of its failure or slow progress and appropriate steps to be taken to avoid wastage and stagnation. Classroom research must also be directed toward developing special curriculum and methods of teaching for the children of the parents of first generation learners, scheduled castes and tribes, and the gifted and differently disabled children.

Secondary Education: Classroom research must be directed toward studying the educational problems of adolescents on the basis of which useful changes could be implemented on the secondary level. The Kothari Education Commission had recommended that secondary education must make efforts in producing trained skilled manpower to take life and vocational needs thereafter. So, studies must concentrate on how far are these objectives being achieved. It must also be studied as to how much the moral education is successful in the character development of students. Research must be conducted to find out the progress and current status of distance education at secondary level, and the need for and effectiveness of alternative schooling strategies.

Higher Education: In the present day India, when the whole world is passing through the revolution of Information Technology, how much and in what way the higher education is contributing, is a very burning and useful topic for research. Serious efforts must be made to study various educational problems of the students in the colleges and universities. In addition to these, library facilities, medium of instruction, curricular reforms, improvement in teaching, women's education, quality assurance and accreditation, research facilities etc. are various problems that must be researched since these have direct impact on the higher education.

Agricultural and Technical Education: The Education Commission recommended that agricultural and technical education should be treated as a part of the general education. Therefore classroom research should be undertaken in this field also to develop the desired curriculum, textbooks, evaluation procedures so that agricultural and technical education can be imparted effectively to the students at different levels.

Non-Formal Education: After determining various psychological, social, and vocational needs of the adult learners, they must be provided by non-formal education through various programmes like, distance education, part-time education, continuing education, adult education, education through mass media, orientation or refresher courses etc. with the help of special instructional material. Research must be conducted on the philosophy, objectives and means of non-formal education, and its effectiveness in fulfilling the needs of present day Indian society.

Teaching Process: No education can educate a person without effective teaching-learning process. The teacher must recognise the individual differences and must be a good academician and psychologist. He/she must be equipped with effective communication skills and teaching skills; and must be imaginative and intelligent enough to clearly understand the needs of the students and the society. His/her teaching must be dynamic enough to suit to present day conditions and needs of the students and the educational climate. Classroom research must also be conducted to explore and develop effective teaching-learning processes.

Education is a boundless field, and is a multidisciplinary subject. Because its content areas can't be strictly and distinctly defined, it is highly difficult to classify educational research. However, this difficulty of classification can be overcome by giving an independent place to all those areas in which some substantial research has been conducted. But there is the problem of classifying research in education since it had an interface with more than one area. So, instead of using unilateral classification system, a multi-classification system should be adopted which enables us to classify a study into more than one area if required. Over 25 areas have been identified in which educational and/or classroom research studies have been conducted by using multiple classification system.

1.5. Development of Educational Research in India

Educational research took birth in India when the Bombay University awarded the first Ph.D. degree in education in 1943 to Dr. D. V. Chickermane for his thesis entitled, "Factor Analysis of

Arithmetical Ability." Since then, there has been considerable growth of educational and/or classroom research all over the nation. However, it was in 1917, when education made its first entry in the university system when a Department of Education was established in the University of Calcutta to study educational problems in a systematic manner.

In 1936 the University of Bombay started M. Ed. Course and in 1943 awarded first Ph. D. degree in education. In 1947, the Government of India, with an objective to providing facilities for educational research at the national level, established the Central Institute of Education (CIE). It was supposed to promote research in educational problems and to offer advanced level training to in-service teachers and other personnel working in the field of education. It was followed by the establishment of the Central Bureau of Textbook Research, and of the Central Bureau of Educational and Vocational Guidance in 1954.

In 1956, the National Institute of Basic Education, and the National Fundamental Centre to work primarily in the field of adult education were established. After these, in 1959, the National Institute of Audio-Visual Education was established which was the sixth institute established in a span of twelve years (1947-1959) to promote educational and/or classroom research.

However, very soon it was realised that these six institutions were working in an independent fashion, and instead of taking education as holistic, these were examining it in fragments. In an order to integrate research, training and extension—the three major components of education - on September 1st, 1961 the National Council of Educational Research and Training (NCERT) was established which very soon became the premier institution for educational and/or classroom research in our country. Although it was established as a central institution, states and Union Territories took it as a model for them and established State Councils of Educational Research and Training (SCERT)/State Institute of Education.

Besides the NCERT, some other national level institutions are also there which are devoted to research in the field of educational problems. Some most important ones are: the UGC, the ICSSR, the National Institute of Educational Planning and Administration (NIEPA, established in 1970), New Delhi, Indian Institute of

Education (IIE, started in 1948), Pune, and Centre of Advanced Study in Education (CASE, established in 1963), Baroda. But amongst all the various institutes, the NCERT is the largest one that acts as a national-level apex body to provide leadership in the formulation of programmes and policy of school education. In addition to these, there are a lot of other institutes, which started by the Government of India or voluntary bodies which occasionally conduct research in the various fields of education.

1.6. Complexities in Educational Research

Even though there is substantial quantitative growth of educational research during the last few decades, though the quality of such studies may be not very high. The reasons of this are also clear: there is a mashroom like growth of degree-giving institutions, more attractive facilities for conducting research, Ph. D. degree being a status symbol and for updating qualifications and getting promotions and higher scales of pay. And naturally, this increase in quantity of research is at the cost of the quality of research. There is a great need to find out the major shortcomings in the field of educational research if we have to maintain the quality in research.

The following are some of the major shortcomings of educational research:

1.6.1. Lack of Clear Educational Perspective

If a nation has to grow, it has to formulate developmental goals on the basis of individual and social needs. And education is the ladder to achieve this. This is regarded as a development-based educational perspective (EP). Studying the educational problems of SC/ST, studying the administration of elementary education in the context of universalisation are some of the examples of research based on a national educational/developmental perspective.

There are non-degree research studies conducted by ICSSR, NIEPA or other bodies. Unlike these research studies, most of the doctoral research lack in this EP, which makes them socially irrelevant and unfruitful. As a result, these types of research, lacking in this perspective, neither throw adequate light on the educational process nor contribute to new knowledge in the field of education - be it theoretical or practical. And that's why educational research in India is unable to influence educational policy, programmes or practices.

1.6.2. Lack of Theoretical Framework

The importance of a sound conceptual and theoretical framework in conducting classroom research is well recognised. Besides helping the researchers to organise the already available empirical findings, it also provides them with the basis for interpreting their own findings in accurate fashion. It guides the researchers in the selection and specific formulation of research problems, in the choice of appropriate educational tools and techniques and also of appropriate designs for analysing the data.

Despite understanding the importance and utility of a sound conceptual framework, it is highly ignored while formulating specific research problems. Researchers show disregard for any theoretical framework in selecting variables of the study and tools and techniques for collecting the data. And this disregard results in very harmful consequences. No doubt, the researcher earn degrees, but at the cost of knowledge.

1.6.3. Insufficient Knowledge about Research Process

Apart from the above-mentioned shortcomings, educational research also suffers from an inadequate comprehension of research process. It is revealed that in the process of selection of problems on an ad hoc basis, there is easy availability of a tool undesirably motivates the future researchers to again and again use the same tool in their research, has also selection of unscientific and unrepresentative samples, gradually decreasing sample size, improper research methodology, inappropriate handling of the data, and in the use of unsuitable statistical techniques. The research process, without adequate understanding, can lead us to nowhere, but will result in the wastage of resources and create harm to the knowledge generation process.

1.6.4. Relevance

A large number of educational research is found to be irrelevant to the national and societal needs. Most of the educational research studies are pure academic exercises and most of these address themselves to the micro level problems, just trying out an easy way to earn a degree. They completely ignore the macro level problems operating in the larger socio-economic context.

1.7. Improving Educational Research

Consistent and honest efforts are to be made by every individual and institution concerned for improving the state of educational research in our country, and this can only be achieved by being a very objective and sensitive researcher. Described below are some suggestions, which may be helpful in improving the status of educational research:

i) *Organisation of educational research:* If the status of educational research is to be improved we will have to begin with the organisation of educational research at institutional level which includes:

   (a) promoting institutional infrastructure,

   (b) fulfilling the need of planned efforts and educational research programmes, and

   (c) developing and maintaining academic leadership.

ii) *Training of researchers:* Ultimately, it is the individual who has to conduct research and the quality of the research largely depends on the abilities of the researcher. Thus, it is of vital importance to provide proper and sincere guidance, training and orientation to those who are going to conduct educational research.

iii) *Dissemination of research:* No research can be useful and fruitful unless the research findings and conclusions are disseminated to practitioners and other related agencies. This can be done by organising national/international level seminars/conferences, publishing the research findings in various journals and magazines for the consumption of interested persons and agencies.

Even though, the educational research endeavour in the country has not failed, but definitely there are clear signs of cracking. This is both due to the internal failings and the external pressures. It is time for the professionals in the field of education to act. First of all, they should try to set their own house straight. It is necessary that concrete actions be taken to mend and improve standards of research in education. At the same time they should also learn to withstand as well as ward off the external pressures through appropriate innovative actions. It is necessary to develop a strong lobby to ensure that planners and administrators do accept educational researchers as respectable partners in the common endeavour to improve education.

1.7.1. Role of NCERT

The National Council of Educational Research and Training (NCERT) supports educational research by providing financial assistance to individuals and outside organisations. It also awards fellowships so that educational problems are investigated and a band of competent research workers is created. Besides supporting the research efforts of others, the Council itself conducts significant research in different areas of. education. The priority areas of research are quality of school life, characteristics of school environment, academic difficulties of students, alternative strategies of education, learning outcomes, value changes, equality of educational opportunity, qualitative improvement of education, etc.

The Council conducts all India educational surveys, provides data processing service, analyses sample data, compiles selected information, collects educational statistics, provides training in survey methods and orientation in sample surveys. It has completed so far four all-India Educational Surveys. During this period, 4th Survey was supplemented by secondary analysis of the data, environmental studies for demography, educational facilities planning studies, district development plans, and the school mapping exercises.

The Council has been concentrating its efforts in identifying the various limiting factors particularly those which relate to the status of women in society and curricular irrelevance which prevent women from taking full benefits of education and facilities. This helps promote education of girls and women. A survey of educational backwardness of girls was taken in the States identified as educationally backward. This project is being funded by UNICEF.

Tools for monitoring and evaluation of universalisation of elementary education programme have been developed during 1981-83 and a pilot try-out conducted. The tools cover enrolment, retention, attendance, transferability from non-format schools, etc. The tools envisage monitoring, physical, academic, teacher, financial and administrative aspects. Monitoring is undertaken at school, block, district, state and national levels. It is done on monthly, quarterly, half-yearly and annual basis.

During these years, the Council undertook evaluation of textbooks at school level from the standpoint of national integration. For this, tools and techniques have been developed, guidelines have been drafted, state agencies have been identified, and textbooks evaluation was taken up in 23 States and Union Territories.

1.7.2. UNICEF Projects

The specific objective of the UNICEF assisted project on Primary Education Curriculum Renewal (since 1975) is to develop innovative need-based curricula, instructional materials and strategies which can satisfy the educational requirements of the underprivileged children of the disadvantaged sections of the society. The project is implemented through 2,465 primary schools and 183 teacher training institutions covering 11,000 teachers and 0.4 million students.

The main objective of the UNICEF-assisted project on Comprehensive Access to Primary Education is to develop for out of-school children of age-group 6-14, a large number of learning materials (episodes) based on local specific problems on modular approach to learning/instruction. The project is being implemented, since 1979, through 974 teacher training institutions and 19 in-service teacher training centres. About 13,000 draft modules have been developed so far.

The specific objective of UNICEF assisted project on Development Activities in Community Education and Participation, since 1975-76, is to develop programmes and instructional materials to provide opportunities of formal and non-formal education to cater to the needs of the age-group 0-3, 3-6, 6-14, 15-35 and others. The project is implemented through 102 community education centres all over India.

UNICEF assisted project on Nutrition, Health, Education and Environmental Sanitation attempts to integrate concepts and practices of nutrition and health education in the curricular programmes of rural schools in 15 centres. It aims at development of environment- based instruction package on nutrition, health education and sanitation for primary school pupils, teacher-educators and supervisor's for more than 2,500 schools.

1.7.3. Role of UGC and other Educational Bodies

During the years 1982 and 1983, the University Grants Commission approved 488 major research projects in science subjects and 54 in humanities and social sciences involving a total grant of Rs. 444.88 lakhs. Besides, the Commission approved 1,880 minor research projects in science and 655 in humanities and social sciences involving an assistance of Rs. 147.32 lakhs.

In the field of Technical Education, five Indian Institutes of Technology, which are apex institutions for engineering education and research, intensified their activities in the areas of continuing education and by starting new inter-disciplinary academic programmes and pursuing research and consultancy services.

The Government of India is directly assisting 12 State Governments and 20 Non-Government institutions for the development of their post-graduate courses as a part of the continuing scheme under the scheme of Development of Post-Graduate Courses and Research Work in Engineering and Technology.

The Review Committee on Post-graduate Education and Research in Engineering and Technology, inter-alia, recommended restructuring and Organisation of Post-graduate courses, identification of emerging areas, revision in the norms of assistance, faculty improvement etc.

The School of Planning and Architecture, with a view to further broadening its academic programmes relating to human settlements and the environment and also to promote research and extension, carried on effectively all its activities/programmes during this period.

The National Institute of Educational Planning and Administration, inter-alia, conducts research and studies and acts as a clearing house of information in the field of educational planning and administration. During the years 1981-83, the Institute took up a number of research studies, besides completing those already in hand.

The Indian Council of Social Science Research promotes and coordinates social science research in the country. The programmes and activities of the council continued during this period. The Council approved a large number of research projects and received completed reports in respect of the projects sanctioned earlier. Besides, the Council continued its support to two sponsored research programmes, and assistance to 17 research institutes in the field of social sciences.

The Indian Council of Historical Research, inter-alia, sponsors historical research programmes. During the period under report, the Council continued to promote and facilitate historical research, which included grant-in-aid programme, sources programme, execution of special projects, holding of seminars, publication of journals/books and collaboration in the field of research. The Council sanctioned several research projects, fellowships and Study-cum-Travel/Contingent grants.

1.8. Conclusion

Education is a process through which a nation molding its future leaders. It doesn't method of learning myriad of textbooks. Instead, it must strengthen the students to spearhead the nation towards prosperity. Valuable researches in the field of education will help to achieve this objective. But researches in India are not adequate to abreast with the international standard. Research is more of a matter of insight, intelligence, extensive knowledge and research skills. For producing high quality research work, the researchers must involve their mind also while conducting a research.

References

Best, John W., *Research in Education*, Englewood Cliffs, New Jersey: Prantice Hall Inc., 1977.

Buch, M. B., *A Survey of Research in Education*, Baroda: CASE, M. S. University, Baroda, 1974.

_______________., *Second Survey of Research in Education (1972-1978)*, Baroda: Society for Educational Research and Development, 1979.

_______________ . and Govinda, R., "Educational Research in India - An Overview", In M. B. Buch (Ed.), *Third Survey of Research in Education* (1978-1983), New Delhi: NCERT, 1987.

_______________ ., "Fourth Survey of Research in Education (1983-1988)", *NCERT*, New Delhi, 1991.

Chandra, S. S. and Sharma, R. K., *Research in Education*, New Delhi: Atlantic Publishers and Distributors, 1997.

Koul, Lokesh, *Methodology of Educational Research*, New Delhi: Vikas Publishing House Pvt. Ltd., 1984.

Monroe, Walters S. ed. *Encyclopaedia of Educational Research*, New York: The MacMillan Company, 1950.

Travers, Robert M. W., *An Introduction to Educational Research*, New York: The MacMillan Company, 1958.

2

Types of Educational Research

2.1. Introduction

Research methods can be restrict under any concrete definitions as it can be classified according to the wish of authors or researchers. Nonetheless, it can generally be classified into basic or applied based on the types of research. However, these are two broad categories into which various types of educational research can be put. According to Travers, "basic (or pure or fundamental) research is designed to add to an organised body of scientific knowledge and does not necessarily produce results of immediate practical value." In basic research, we generally emphasise the formulation and testing of a theory and discovery of the knowledge only for the sake of the knowledge. In the field of education, basic research attempts at the development and testing of the theories of the behaviour of learners and teachers in educational and/or classroom settings.

On the other hand, applied (or even action) research attempts at solving any specific problem of some immediate practical value to society or any institution/organisation. According to Travers, "applied research is undertaken to solve an immediate practical problem and the goal of adding to scientific knowledge is secondary." In addition to possessing most of the characteristics of basic research, it also applies scientific method of inquiry. In fact, these two are not distinct, and involve each other. Methods of research may be put in various classifications such as:

— *Application*: Basic research or applied research.

— *Purpose*: Description, generalisation, prediction, determination of causes, etc.

— *Place where the research is to be conducted*: Field research or laboratory research.

— *Data collection devices*: Tests, questionnaires, interviews, schedules, etc.

— *Nature of the collected data*: Qualitative, quantitative, objective, subjective, etc.

— *The field to which applied*: Education, psychology, biology, etc.

These classifications are not exclusive and may overlap with each other on some common point of view. Hence, it is appropriate to categorise various types of research methods in terms of the kinds of information and knowledge they deliver. The types of educational researches are:

i. Historical Research
ii. Descriptive Research
iii. Correlational Research
iv. Causal-Comparative Research
v. Experimental Research
vi. Action Research
vii. Field Level Research

2.2. Historical Research

History is a meaningful record of human achievement. It is not merely a list of chronological events but a truthful integrated account of the relationships between persons, events, times and places. We use history to understand the past and to try to understand the present in light of past events and developments.

Historical research emphasises on and describes what was . In historical research, we very carefully and critically investigate, record, analyse and interpret the past so that we may be able to uncover the hidden facts which may enable us to understand the past as well as the present, and if possible, to predict or anticipate the future in the light of that past.

2.2.1. Historical Research in Education

Conducting historical research in education can be of immense importance for both the theoretical and the practical purposes. The findings of historical research may help us in learning from past mistakes and discoveries, we may identify the educational areas that need reform, and, if possible, we may predict the future trend of any given phenomenon. The importance of historical research in education can be explained as:

— Knowledge of the history of schools and other educational agencies is an important part of the professional training of the teacher or the school administrator.

— Much of the work of the school is traditional. The nature of the work of the teacher and the school administrator is restrictive and tends to foster prejudices in favour of familiar methods. The history of education is the "sovereign solvent" of educational prejudices.

— The history of education enables the educational worker to detect fads and frills in whatever form they may appear, and it serves as a necessary preliminary to educational reform.

— Only in the light of their origin and growth can the numerous educational problems of the present be viewed sympathetically and without bias by the teacher, the school administrator, or the public.

— The history of education shows how the functions of social institutions shift and how the support and control of education have changed from very simple and local arrangements to those that are now somewhat centralised and complex.

— The history of education is an ally in the scientific study of education rather than a competition. It serves to present the educational ideals and standards of other times, and it enables social workers to avoid mistakes of the past.

— It inspires respect for sound scholarship and reverence for great teachers.

2.2.2 Areas of Historical Research in Education

The areas coming under historical research in education are:

i) General history of education

ii) History of educational planning and policy

iii) History of major branches of education

iv) History of educational systems

v) History of contemporary problems in education

vi) History of philosophy and methodology of education

vii) History of literature in education

viii) Legislative history of education

ix) History of innovations in education

x) History of institutions or organisations of educational importance.

These are some very broad areas, and the interested researcher must extract some solvable problem from any of these areas.

2.2.3. Steps in Historical Research

Steps to conduct historical research are:

i) *Selection of the Problem:* As per interest, the researcher may select any problem regarding the history of teaching practices, curriculum, educational concepts and thoughts, institutions/organisations of educational importance, etc. A review of the literature provided by other educationists and historians, and/or experts' opinion, are very helpful and useful in selecting and defining our problem.

ii) *Formulation of Hypothesis:* Hypothesis (or hypotheses) guides us in solving our problem in historical research by focusing our attention to the tentative solutions, and by preventing us from a blind search. In historical research, hypotheses are not always explicit. Like other kinds of research, we confirm or do not confirm (or retain or reject) our hypotheses as the case may be. In testing our hypotheses, we may collect the evidence from a lot of sources like individuals, books, schools, etc., as is required by our particular research problem.

iii) *Data Collection:* It is a necessary condition in all types of research that the researcher must collect relevant and accurate data so that the hypotheses may be correctly verified. In historical research, the data collection process is very time consuming and tedious. The researcher must be skillful enough so that he/she may select the relevant data, pertinent to his/her problem, from the vast ocean of available literature or various sources from where the data emerge. The sources of data are:

   a) *Primary sources of data:* These data provide first hand information from direct measurement, eyewitness accounts or observations. These data are actually collected by the researcher through questionnaires and schedules, and by using the method of observation and interview techniques.

   b) *Secondary sources of data:* Secondary data refer simply to the second-hand data. The good examples of secondary sources are most of the published or unpublished material, reports, personal diaries, letters, books and encyclopaedias. It should be noted that the reliability and truthfulness of such information is questionable. So, the secondary data should not be regarded as much reliable and dependable and the researcher should critically verify it from other sources also if possible and available.

iv) *Research Tools:* These are the instruments that are required to collect data from the subjects (subjects refer to the living organisms whom we study in the research; or, the 'respondents'). In historical research, we frequently make use of interview, questionnaires, observation, and different standardised tests.

v) *Criticism of the Data:* After the data collection is over, it is subjected to rigorous evaluation, which, in other words, is called as 'criticism of the data.' The truthfulness of the data and credibility of the source of the information is questionable; so, the researcher should critically evaluate his/her data and the sources of the data. The types criticism of the data are:

a) *External criticism:* Here, the source of the data comes under the critical evaluation.

b) *Internal criticism:* Here, we critically evaluate the content of the data.

vi) *Treatment or Analysis of the Data:* In historical research, data may be treated or analysed in any one or more of the following methods:

a) *Simple presentation of the data:* In this type of data analysis, no statistical procedures are applied on the data, and the collected information is presented as it is.

b) *Data conversion:* Here, we may apply simple statistics on the data like mean, median, or percentages, as appropriate, just to make the data more meaningful and comparable. We may use graphs also for clear and easy presentation of the data.

c) *Further statistical treatment:* Simple summarising method is inadequate to find out differences between or among the groups. In such cases, still higher statistical techniques like standard deviation, chi-square, analysis of variance, etc can be used.

vii) *Interpretation:* In historical research, findings may be interpreted in the light of either the status or the differences between or among the investigated groups. This is very helpful in not only understanding the past but also in comparing the past with the present. It also gives due weightage to the trends and causes that emphasise 'the changes' that have taken place progressively, over a period of time. It helps us a lot in 'decision making' regarding preparing better curriculum, etc. But, the interpretation of historical data is not as simple and easy as it seems to be; rather it requires a lot of skills and expertise.

viii) *Report Writing:* The last and most important step of a research process is to write the concise, to-the-point and well-organised report of that research. The report of an historical research includes statement of the problem, brief review of the pertinent literature, procedure of the data collection, actual source(s) of the data, criticism of the data, treatment, analysis and interpretation of the data, the conclusions drawn and references/bibliography. Although the reports of the historical research are criticised for being comparatively dull and uninteresting, the researcher should use all of his/her creativity and expertise to make it precise and interesting without using flowery language.

2.3. Descriptive Research

Descriptive research can be of two types:

i. Quantitative descriptive research emphasises on what is, and makes use of quantitative methods to describe, record, analyse and interpret the present conditions.

ii. Qualitative descriptive research also emphasises on what is, but makes use of non-quantitative research methods in describing the conditions of the present.

Sometimes referred to as non-experimental or correlational research, descriptive research studies the relationships among non-manipulated variables only. In this type of research, the investigator selects the relevant variables from the events/conditions that have already occurred or exist at present, and analyses their relationship without introducing any manipulations to the variables.

In descriptive research, we study the events or human behaviour in natural settings, because sometimes it would be difficult to manipulate the variables, and because sometimes it is unethical. For example, if you want to study the effect of smoking on the chances of cancer development, it would be totally unethical to deliberately assign subjects in the group that will smoke and in that who will not so that a comparative study could be done. So, this and other types of relationships between and among the variables are studied under natural conditions of the classroom, home, factory, offices, etc. Because of its ease in use, descriptive research is the most popular and widely used method in educational research. The descriptive research method is easy to use because in this method, the research data can be very easily obtained and interpreted. The results of descriptive research provide us with a platform to make important decisions and also generate more research ideas to be tested by the future researchers.

2.3.1 Purpose of Descriptive Research

The broad purpose of descriptive research in `Education' is to study the present problems of the students, teachers, administration, curriculum, teaching learning process, and the like, and to suggest some solutions to these problems.

2.3.2. Importance of Descriptive Research

The following points prove the significance of descriptive research in the field of education:

i) *Description of the Present:* The descriptive research studies describe the current and present educational phenomena, problems and/or opinions possessed by the teachers, students, etc. about their educational environment or scenario.

ii) *Easy and Direct:* This method is very easy and direct in use and, hence, is a very popular and widely used research method.

iii) *Only Means:* Many times we find the manipulation of the variables a tough job. Therefore, we use this method in which we study the existing relationship between or among the variables without any manipulation.

iv) *Suggesting Solutions:* Descriptive research not only describes the current problem but also many times suggests valuable solutions to the educational problems.

v) *Developing Data Collection Tools:* The descriptive research is also very useful and helpful in developing the data collection tools like questionnaires, schedules, checklists, etc.

vi) *Development of Generalisations, Principles or Theories:* By dealing with the relationships between or among the variables, the descriptive research is also very useful in developing new generalisations, principles or theories which possess universal validity and utility.

2.3.3. Types of Descriptive Research

Descriptive research can be divided into:

2.3.3.1. Survey

The term survey is derived from two words: 'Sur' or 'Sor,' which means "over" and 'Veeir' or 'vor,' which means, "to see." Accordingly, the term survey means to look over or to oversee. In survey, we collect the data from a large number of people at some particular time about some particular phenomenon. It is a very skillful activity that not only requires imaginative and expert planning of the study, but also accurate data collection, careful analysis and logical interpretation of the collected data, and intelligent reporting of the results and conclusions.

Surveys can further be of many types:

i) *School Survey:* The main purpose of a school survey is to judge the overall effectiveness of the school programme and suggest some improvement if and where necessary. The very first formal survey was conducted in 1910 of the school of Boise, Idaho (USA), and now a days it has become the necessity of each nation and state to evaluate the effectiveness of its schools as a functional unit.

ii) *Job Survey*: It mainly refers to job analysis. In the field of education, in job surveys, we collect relevant information about the general and specific duties and responsibilities of the teachers, non-teaching staff and administrative personnel, the working conditions in which they work, the nature and type of facilities they enjoy, etc. These types of information will further help the employers and administrators to improve their working conditions so that jobs must become so attractive and remunerative that they will attract the right people for the right types of jobs at the right time.

iii) *Documentary Survey:* It closely relates to historical research since in such surveys we study the existing documents. But it is different from historical research in which our emphasis was on the study of the past; and in the descriptive research we emphasised on the study of the present. Descriptive research in the field of education may focus on describing the existing school practices, attendance rate of the students, health records, etc.

iv) *Public Opinion Survey:* Sometimes, by the help of questionnaires or interviews, we collect the public opinion on various educational issues like implementation of co-education at school or college level, privatization of education, etc. These help us know what the public thinks about our selected topic on the basis of which we might take important and crucial decisions.

v) *Social Surveys:* These are also known as community surveys. Since there is very close relationship between the school and the community, researchers often conduct community surveys to determine the educational needs of a particular society or to assess and enhance the schools' performance for the benefit of the society at large.

2.3.3.2. *Correlational Studies*

In this type of studies we determine the extent to which two variables are correlated, the direction of their correlation (positive or negative), and whether the correlation (represented by the letter r) is significant or not. In any direction (positive or negative), variables may be highly, moderately or lowly correlated, or they may not be correlated at all (i.e. zero correlation). One very simple example of a correlational study in the field of education may be to study the correlation between teacher reinforcement and student performance.

2.3.3.3. *Causal-comparative Studies*

This is a type of research in educational studies in which we suggest the cause and effect or we suggest what causes the other thing, e.g. high motivational level causes better performance. But this type of research possesses a serious limitation in that it cannot manipulate the causes (or independent variables) to prove this suggested relationship.

2.3.3.4. *Developmental Studies*

These types of descriptive studies deal with the changes that take place as a function of time.

2.3.4. Steps in Descriptive Research

The steps followed in descriptive research are almost similar to the ones followed in other forms of research. Following are the steps adopted in describing and interpreting the existing conditions:

2.3.4.1. *Selection of the Problem*

A researcher, from the area of his/her interest, may select any problem to study the existing conditions or phenomena. He/she should clearly state the problem and define the variables in operational terms.

2.3.4.2. *Formulation of Hypothesis*

The research hypothesis guides us throughout the research process in solving our research problems. We should formulate the hypotheses on the basis of the existing theories and facts.

2.3.4.3. *Identification of Data*

It is necessary to identify the appropriate type of (qualitative or quantitative) data to be collected so that our hypothesis may be correctly tested.

2.3.4.4. *Selection or Development of a Research Tool*

After deciding the nature of the data to be collected, it becomes easy for us to select the appropriate measurement tool and if any standardised tool of our interest is not available we have to develop our own tool as per our research requirements.

2.3.4.5. *Sample Selection*

While selecting the sample to be studied, we must choose a representative sample and apply randomization techniques in sample selection, if possible.

2.3.4.6. *Data Collection*

After finalising the tools to be used and sample to be studied, we begin our actual data collection.

2.3.4.7. Treatment or Analysis of the Data

The data collected is then treated with the appropriate statistical techniques.

2.3.4.8. Interpretation

While interpreting our obtained findings we should also emphasize the existing theories and interpret our results in their light. We should also see if our findings build a new theory or conform to the old ones.

2.3.4.9. Report Writing

It is the last and most important step of a research study, i.e. to write an appropriate and clear report of what we have done and found, so that people may also take advantage of this new knowledge.

2.4. Correlational Research

The main aim of educational research is not only to discover what is presently unknown but also to predict the future relationships between various variables. These predictions are comparatively easy and possible to be made if we explore the existing strong relationships between certain variables.

The major aim of a correlational research is to explore the correlation between or among the variables. These correlations help us better understand the conditions and events in a meaningful way, and in making predictions about the future conditions and events. These research studies ultimately enable us to explain, predict and, up to some extent, control certain conditions and events.

In the educational settings, correlational research is targeted toward the following four broad categories of topics:

- Researching various human traits related to learning, viz. personality, motivation, intelligence, etc.
- Researching various classroom conditions related to learning, viz. class size, teacher behaviour, peer interaction, etc.
- Researching various teaching practices, procedures, and materials related to learning.

— Researching the validation of educational tests and measurements.

2.4.1. Sources of Data

Actually, correlational research requires only a few sources of data, but these sources must provide or supply two measures or scores for each subject studied. For example, if we want to explore the relationship between the level of anxiety and student performance, we essentially need scores on these two variables each for all the subjects of the sample.

2.4.2. Types of Correlations

We require pairs of test scores for each subject to calculate correlation between these pairs. But the nature of these pairings (or data obtained) requires us to calculate correlation by any of the following different methods of correlation:

Pearson r: It is the most commonly used correlational procedure. In this, we need pairs of raw scores on two tests, one pair for each subject of the sample, e.g. marks obtained by a student in the tests of science and math.

Spearman r: Sometimes we cannot obtain raw scores but we obtain the ranking of the subjects. Then, we have to calculate Spearman's rank order correlation. For example, to explore the relationship between self-confidence and leadership we shall have to use this method. Here we may be unable to obtain the raw scores of the subjects on these two variables but we may rank them on these.

Biserial r: It is calculated when we have scores of the subjects on one variable or trait, but on the second variable, we have to put them into a dichotomy (dichotomous means 'cut into two parts'), which means that we have to place them in either this or another category. For example, we may plan to explore the relationship between mental age (M.A., a measurable variable into scores) and number of parents in the family (dichotomous variable-either one parent i.e. either mother or father or two i.e. both mother and father).

Tetrachoric r: In biserial r, we have one continuous variable (expressed in test scores) and second dichotomous variable (a two-fold classification). But sometimes we may get both the variables dichotomous (or a 2 x 2 or four-fold table). Then we have to compute tetrachoric r. Here our both variables are not measured in scores but are capable of being separated into two categories. For example, we may wish to discover the relationship between intelligence (above average/below average) and self-confidence (above average/below average). Here we have, as per our research objectives, decided to study the relationship between two categories of intelligence and two categories of self-confidence.

Partial Correlation: In correlational approach, mostly the third variable problem refrains us from drawing inferences on the basis of the observed r between two variables. According to Christensen, "the third variable problem refers to the fact that the two variables may be correlated not because they are causally related but because some third variable caused both of them." For example, it is found that reading ability and vocabulary are highly correlated, but, in fact, both of these variables are strongly affected by intelligence. Hence, if anybody wants to study the actual correlation between these two variables, he must first partial out the effect of intelligence which is done by the method of partial correlation.

2.4.3. Research Tools

In correlational research, we require data in the form of numbers, rankings or dichotomies. To obtain these types of data, as per our research design, we may use "standardised tests" (like intelligence tests), "other measuring devices" (e.g., heart beat, pulse rate, etc), or "established criteria" (to be used in making rankings and dichotomies).

2.4.4. Steps in Correlational Research

The correlational research is very simple and uncomplicated to conduct. It involves the following steps, most of which you will find a little bit similar to other research methods:

2.4.4.1. Selecting and Defining a Problem

Like other types of research, correlational research also requires first of all a researcher to select and define his/her research problem. Here the researcher should select at least "two variables" (one can select even more).

2.4.4.2. *Formulating Hypothesis*

Generally, null hypothesis is formulated in correlational research because it seems much easier to reject a null hypothesis than to retain a research hypothesis. It simply states, "No relationship exists between A and B."

2.4.4.3. *Data Collection*

As per the nature of the variables, the next step of this research method is to collect the data in pairings of scores, rankings, or groupings by applying the appropriate research tools.

2.4.4.5. *Data Compilation*

After collecting the data, we must next compile it in such a way that two measures (i.e. scores, rankings, or groupings) can be shown for each subject of the sample.

2.4.4.6. *Analysis and Interpretation of Data*

Treat the data statistically by applying appropriate correlational technique to compute the correlation between the two sets of scores. Then we interpret our findings in the light of (i) the size of the correlation, (ii) the direction of the correlation (positive or negative), and (iii) its significance level.

i) *The Size of the Correlation:* The degree or size or strength of the relationship between two variables is expressed by the coefficient of correlation. Whether positive or negative, the more the coefficient the stronger or closer the relationship. It should be noted that, irrespective of the correlational procedures followed, the range of the coefficient lies in between 0 (means no relationship at all) to 1.00 (means perfect correlation). However, in research, these values of 0 and/or 1.00 are never or rarely obtained.

ii) *The Direction of the Correlation*: You can find the two variables correlated in either positive or negative direction. The direction of the correlation is independent of the size of the correlation, and both have nothing to do with each other. Correlations of +.62 and -.62 are of exactly the identical size but show a different type of relationship (the former is positive correlation and the latter shows negative correlation). Positive correlations indicate that increase or decrease in one variable tends to accompany the increase or decrease in another variable in parallel fashion. If, on the other hand, increase in one variable tends to decrease in another and vice versa, it indicates a negative correlation. The higher or lower the correlation (either positive or negative), the more accurately we can predict one variable from the other.

iii) *Significance Level of Correlation*: And, as far as the significance level of obtained correlation is concerned, we first compute the standard error (SE) of the correlation and then multiply this SE by 1.96 (for .05 level of significance) or by 2.56 (for .01 level of significance). The obtained correlation is considered significant if it is larger than the value obtained by the multiplication of SE with either 1.96 or 2.56.

2.4.4.7. Report Writing

This is, as in other types of research, the last step of a correlational research in which we very skillfully and logically report our problem, variables, hypothesis, results of the study, analysis and interpretation of the findings in terms of coefficients, direction and significance of the correlation obtained between or among the variables.

2.5. Casual-Comparative Research

Causal-comparative research-a type of descriptive research-is also referred to as "ex post facto" research, which means after the fact or from a thing done afterwards. This simply implies that the researcher is studying the cause-effect relationship that already exists, without attempting any control or change in either the cause or the effect. In other words, it refers to some type of subsequent action taken after something has occurred or happened, and how we want to study or evaluate its effect in terms of the causal relationship.

According to Kerlinger, "Ex post facto research is systematic empirical inquiry in which the scientist does not have direct control of independent variables because their manifestations have already occurred or because they are inherently not manipulabe. Inferences about relations among variables are made, without direct intervention, from concomitant variation of independent and dependent variables." Thus, in this type of research, we are unable to control or manipulate the causes or independent variables and now we simply try to explore how and why are they related to the effects or the dependent variables. Although this method also studies cause and effect relationship, yet it is technically different from experimental research in which we prove this cause-effect relationship by manipulating the independent variables. But, in causal-comparative research, it is neither possible nor practical to manipulate the cause because genetics, time or circumstances fix it. And, thus, we have to logically establish the cause-effect relationship, we cannot prove it "experimentally." For example, if we wish to study the delinquency, we cannot manipulate the causes of delinquency.

The causal-comparative research is based upon John Stuart Mill's method of exploring causal relationships. According to Mill's Method of Agreement, "If two or more instances of the phenomenon under investigation have only one circumstances in common, the circumstance in which alone all the instances agree, is the cause (or effect) of the given phenomena."

Actually, this research begins with the observation of any dependent variable or the effect. Then, the researcher starts exploring the possible independent variables or causes that may be related to that dependent variable.

No doubt, the experimental method is the best, but in many situations we find it impractical or costly in terms of time, money and efforts. Also, in some other situations, ethical considerations may not permit a researcher to use experimental method. D. B. Van Dalen rightly remarks that, "Respect for living things, prevents an investigator from inflicting unnecessary pain, hardship, or harm on others, or from interfering in any way with the normal growth and development of an individual." Here then, we have to make use of causal-comparative research. Most of the educational research studies employ the method of causal-comparative research since, in education, the independent variables are often difficult or impossible to manipulate or control. This method helps us study the problems that cannot be investigated under laboratory controls and provide valuable information about the causal relationships between two events.

2.5.1. Steps in Causal-Comparative Research

Although steps involved in causal-comparative research do not differ much from steps involved in other types of research, yet some points are to be taken care of while conducting a causal-comparative research. These are given as follows:

2.5.1.1. Selection of a Problem

In causal-comparative research, you should select such a problem, the independent variables of which can neither be manipulated nor be controlled.

2.5.1.2. Formulation of the Hypothesis

Mostly, the hypotheses are stated in the null form in causal-comparative research.

2.5.1.3. Data and Tools

Generally, in causal-comparative research, we collect biographical data, because our main purpose here is to detect past causes for the present effects or behaviour patterns. And, as far as tools are concerned, so as to find out the causal factors we may use standardised tests, questionnaires, schedules, interviews, observation, etc.

2.5.1.4. Data Analysis

After measuring the existing dependent variable of groups of subjects, we may then test the differences between the groups for significance through 'difference between means' (or t test),' or may apply chi-square or analysis of variance.

2.5.1.5. Data Interpretation

If your data reveal that both the different groups actually differ on the dependent variable, you may interpret it as a causal relationship between your selected cause and effect. Here, you must provide logical arguments to build your case to be strong- that this particular effect is the result of this particular cause. For effective interpretation, you may do the following:

i) Provide suitable and relevant examples which show that without this cause, the effect could not have occurred.

ii) Show whether, to produce this effect, your identified cause is sufficient or enough by itself.

iii) Show whether there are some other conditions also that could be equally responsible for causing of this particular effect.

2.5.1.6. *Derive Findings*

Although, as it is clear till now, you can do nothing to manipulate or control the causes, yet finding causal relationships is highly beneficial because it enables us to anticipate, adapt to, and make provisions for the future "effects."

2.5.1.7. *Report Writing*

You might have noted that causal-comparative research requires highly skillful and careful steps to be taken during the research process. It is also required while writing your research report which is the last step of the research process.

2.5.2 Limitations of Causal-comparative Research

These studies suffer from the following limitations that are difficult to remove:

— We lack controls in causal-comparative research.

— Identification of relevant causes is difficult.

— Generally, causes are multiple rather than single.

— Causes may differ from situation to situation for the same effect.

— Even after establishing a relationship between variables, it becomes difficult to determine which is the cause and which is the effect.

— Selecting subjects and assigning them to dichotomous categories is also very difficult.

Despite all these limitations, causal-comparative research is very useful, and a good substitute of experimental studies, where we cannot manipulate or control the independent variables and we have to establish some causal relationship between or among the variables.

2.6. Experimental Research

Experimental research is the description and analysis of what will be or what will occur, under carefully controlled conditions. As far as the purpose and procedures of research are concerned, causal-comparative research and experimental research are almost alike. But, there is one very important difference that separates them. This difference is regarding the cause. In causal-comparative research the cause cannot be manipulated; on the other hand, in experimental research, we can and do manipulate the causes so as to change the effects. The most reliable and dependable type of educational research is the experimental research that involves "experimentation", or that we conduct "experiments" to explore the true causal relatiuonships.

"Experiment" simply refers to the process of studying the effect of independent variable(s) on dependent variable under controlled conditions. Thus, in the experimental method, we manipulate one or more causes and study what type of changes this manipulation has caused in the effects. But, to explore the true relationship between these independent and dependent variables (i.e. cause and effect), we have to control extraneous variables that might pollute or distort our research findings and conclusions.

2.6.1. Nature of Experimental Research

The four inevitable characteristics of experimental research are:

2.6.1.1. Control

In experimental research our main purpose of control is to create such an environment or situation (mostly in the laboratory) so that the effects of our desired variables can be measured objectively. By control, we have to reduce the effect of extraneous variables to the minimum, if we cannot completely remove it.

2.6.1.2. Manipulation

Unlike the descriptive research, in which one observes the naturally occurring phenomena, in experimental research we deliberately manipulate the independent variables (or experimental variables or treatment variables). By increasing or decreasing or removing it, we study what happens to the dependent variables.

2.6.1.3. Observation

In an experiment, we intelligently manipulate the independent variables and carefully observe and record the effects of this manipulation on the dependent variables or some measurable behaviour of our sample.

2.6.1.4. Replication

Despite all the objective and careful efforts of the researcher to control the effects of extraneous variables, still some remain unidentified and uncontrolled and then influence his/her research findings and conclusions. These and other discrepancies, if any, can be taken care of and removed through logically replicating the study.

2.6.2. Experimental Research in Education

The experiment is the only means for settling disputes regarding educational practice, the only way of verifying educational improvements, and the only way of establishing a cumulative tradition in which improvements can be introduced without the danger of a faddish discard of old wisdom in favour of inferior novelties.

By conducting educational experiments we may determine and evaluate the accuracy, adequacy and effectiveness of various educational programmes and strategies. On the basis of this we may further conduct experiments to explore the possibilities for the effective formulation of proper educational planning and execution and, if needed, for modification in the existing educational policies, programmes, and teaching practices, etc.

2.6.3. Steps in Experimental Research

The steps involved in experimental research are almost similar to those of a scientific method, the brief description of which is as follows:

2.6.3.1. Survey of the Latest Literature

The first and foremost step of an experimental research is to up-to-date our knowledge about our problem area. Survey of the latest literature acquaints us with what has been done till now in our area and what is to be or should be done further.

2.6.3.2. Selecting, Defining and Delimiting our Problem

After surveying the literature, we should select a problem that is solvable, researchable, significant, novel and of practical importance. Also, we should operationally define our variables.

Variable: A variable is a characteristic that has different values or levels among the subjects of the sample, e.g. height, weight, intelligence, skills, personality, memory, etc. Mainly there are three types of variables.

Independent Variable: It is also known as the experimenter's variable because he/she manipulates it to explore the effects of this manipulation on the subjects to be studied, e.g. levels of motivation, teaching methods, etc.

Dependent Variable: It is the variable of the subjects that is influenced by the manipulation of the independent variable. It is the behaviour of the subjects or the outcome that the researcher wants to measure, e.g. degree of learning as might be effected by the motivation level or teaching methods.

Extraneous Variable: These are those variables that are neither manipulated by the experimenter nor he/she is interested to study their effect on dependent variable, or their relationships with the dependent variables. Yet, these, if not identified and controlled, cast significant influence on the dependent variable (or on the behaviour of the subjects or on the outcome), e.g. students' level of intelligence. If the level of intelligence is not controlled in an experiment, it may influence the effect of teaching method (or motivation level) on learning.

2.6.3.3. *Stating the Hypothesis*

An experiment is regarded as a process of testing the hypothesis. On the basis of the existing literature, we formulate our research hypotheses that guide us throughout the research process.

2.6.3.4. *Preparing Research Plan and Design*

Research design is a type of blueprint that guides us how to conduct an experiment. According to D. B. Van Dalen, we decide the following in preparing the experimental plan:

- Identify all the extraneous variables and determine how you are going to control them.
- Select a proper and appropriate research design. For a detailed study of research designs, you may consult Christensen, Koul or any other available book on research methodology.
- Select a representative sample (preferably through randomisation procedures), assign subjects (again randomly) to experimental or control groups, and assign experimental treatments to the groups as per your research design. Here, a great care should be taken that your groups should be as similar as possible in all significant ways, except for the differences you are interested in to measure.
- Select a research instrument or construct and validate your own, if already standardised tools or instrument is not available, to measure your particular dependent variable.
- Outline data collection procedures and, if possible, conduct some pilot work to detect various shortcomings of your design or sample etc. at an earlier stage so that you may make essential modifications in it.

2.6.3.5. *Data Collection*

After finalising the research plan and design, the next step is to actually conduct the experiment and measure the dependent variable. Here the data come from the primary sources.

2.6.3.6. *Data Analysis and Interpretation*

After collecting the data, like other research methods, we classify, tabulate and analyse our data by applying appropriate statistical techniques. Then, we interpret our findings and draw relevant conclusions on the basis of which we retain or reject, prove or disprove, our research hypothesis.

2.6.3.7. *Conclusions and Generalisation*

We must restrict our conclusions to the population only that we actually studied, and we must not over-generalise the findings in respect to both the population and the situation studied.

2.6.3.8. *Report Writing*

Lastly, like other research methods, we report what we have obtained and concluded through writing a research report skillfully, logically and objectively.

2.6.4. Advantages of Experimental Method

Following are the important advantages of experimental research over other research methods:

2.6.4.1. *Establishing Direction of Causality*

It was a shortcoming of causal-comparative research that although we establish some causal relationship between variables, yet we could not determine the direction of causality due to our inability in manipulating the causes. In experimental research, on the other hand, we can and we do manipulate the variables. Hence, we can determine the direction of this causal relationship between the cause and effect.

i) *Controlled Conditions and Situations:* In an experiment, conditions are under our complete control, and we may manipulate these as per our research objectives.

ii) *Reliable and Valid:* Experimental method leads us to the reliable data and valid conclusions and generalizations.

iii) *Objective and Scientific:* Experimental method is objective and scientific. In this method, we try to control our personal biases, prejudices, and extraneous variables that, in turn, provide us with the objective data.

iv) *Controlling Future Events:* Findings of the experimental research also enable us to control future events.

v) *Possibility and Replication:* If you want to replicate the study and verify the previous findings, experimental method fully permits you for this critical replication of a study.

2.6.5. Limitations and Disadvantages of Experiments

Besides the above advantages, experimental research possesses the following limitations also:

2.6.5.1. *Difficult to Control Variables*

The nature of social and educational phenomena is very complex and it is difficult to completely control all types of variables in an experiment.

i) *Lengthy and Costly:* The process of experimentation is comparatively lengthy and costly also because in it you essentially need a well-equipped laboratory.

ii) *Artificiality:* Because of the imposed controls of various types in the laboratory, the behaviour of the subjects does not remain natural, and we might be studying the 'artificial' behaviour.

iii) *Difficulty in Creating Certain Conditions:* Not all types of situations can be created in a laboratory-like true emotions of fear, sadness, happiness etc. Also, the ethical considerations restrict us from creating certain conditions in laboratory to study their effects on the behaviour of the subjects.

iv) *Cooperation of the Subjects:* We need true and honest cooperation of our subjects in an experiment that is often difficult to receive.

v) *Experimenter's Biases:* Above all, an experimenter also is a human being with all the shortcomings and biases. It is also equally difficult to control the experimenter's biases, feelings and prejudices completely, and these may have adverse effects on the results of the study.

However, these limitations do not lessen the importance of experimental method. Being the most scientific among other research methods, this is the most reliable, widely respected and widely used method of research.

2.7. Action Research

The field of education has shown great interest in action research since the 1930s. In 1926, Buckingham used the concept of action research in education for the first time in his book 'Research for Teachers', but the credit goes to Stephen M. Corey for using this concept for the first time in the field of studying and solving educational problems. Applied research is also referred to as action research.

In the field of educational research, thus, action research is an applied research that the teachers, instructors and school administrators conduct to tackle and deal with classroom problems and improving their classroom practices. We may conduct studies in order to explore the possibilities of improving our school and classroom practices, the professional as well as personal growth and development of a teacher, developing better curriculum and preparing better textbooks. Best and Kahn write, "its purpose is to improve school practices and, at the same time, to improve those who try to improve the practices: to combine the research processes, habits of thinking, ability to work harmoniously with others, and professional spirit."

It is worth noting that action research is a research conducted through direct action and is primarily focused on immediate application, not on the development of broad theories or generalisations or on general application. It studies the problem from the point of view of here and now in one's local setting and its findings are evaluated in terms of local applicability, not in terms of universal applicability and validity. In the field of education, NCERT has been taking special interests to promote action research through seminars and workshops, etc. to impart knowledge and skills required for action research.

2.7.1. Characteristics of Action Research

Action research can be characterised as follows :

- It is a scientific process for studying and solving the current practical problems of education.
- It is a personal research carried out for clinical utility.
- Only the practitioner can study the problem in a better way.

— It focuses on improving and modifying the current practices.
— Instead of contributing to the gamut of theoretical knowledge, it studies the educational problems in terms of local applicability in the local settings of a practitioner.

2.7.2. Objectives of Action Research

The following are the major objectives of action research:

— To identify problem areas and improve the working conditions of a school.
— To develop scientific attitude among teachers, students, principals, and administrators for studying, understanding, and solving their current academic problems.
— To bring potential of excellence in school functionaries.
— To help in making the environment of the school more conducive to learning.
— To raise the performance and aspiration level of the students by generating a healthy environment for learning.

2.7.3. Steps in Action Research

In an order to solve the day-to-day school problems, every teacher makes some sort of working experimentation though these are not scientific and, hence, cannot be considered as action research. So, it implies that action research is scientific and contains all the elements of the scientific method. Following steps may be followed in conducting action research:

2.7.3.1. *Identification and Selection of a Problem*

A teacher may identify and select a problem regarding his/her teaching, examinations, extra-curricular activities, and about administration and organization of his/her institution. In identifying the problem area, he/she should be sensitive, objective and practical enough.

2.7.3.2. *Defining and Delimiting the Problem*

The next step is to define our problem in terms of actions to be taken and goals to be achieved. We should also delimit our problem by localising it in terms of class, subject, section, and period in which the teacher is facing some problem.

2.7.3.3. Analysing the Causes of the Problem

Next, various possible causes of that particular problem are specified and analysed in the light of sufficient evidence which show some logical relationship of the causes with the problem. This way, we enlist various causes which are fundamentally responsible for the existence of that problem.

2.7.3.4. Formulation of Hypothesis

Formulation of a hypothesis is considered an essential and important research step since it guides the researcher in the investigation of unknown facts and theories. In action research also, we formulate action hypothesis on the basis of the assumed causes of the problem.

2.7.3.5. Research Design

A research design is prepared before starting actual data collection on the basis of which we may either establish or disprove our hypothesis. The nature of the design in action research is flexible and can be changed at any time as per the demands of the situations or the convenience of the researcher. It consists of method, sample and the techniques of data collection.

2.7.3.6. Data Collection

As per the design we have finalised, we begin our actual data collection with the help of research tools we have selected, like questionnaires, interview, observation, etc. We record and score the responses of the subjects.

2.7.3.7. Analysis and Interpretation of Data

After tabulating the data, we apply appropriate and relevant statistical techniques to the data for analysing them so that we may be able to take some logical decision about our hypothesis.

2.7.3.8. *Drawing Conclusions/Speculations*

On the basis of the obtained results, we draw appropriate and logical conclusions in the form of some new knowledge, information, and solution for the practical problems. Here, the researcher may be able to further hypothesize/predict about what is likely to occur in the studied problem area.

2.7.3.9. *Intervening*

The next and most important step of an action research involves changing the practice or previous classroom approach in response to the conclusions we have just drawn. Here, we concentrate on testing our recent hypothesis about the solution that we have just suggested on the basis of a practical study.

2.7.3.10. *Observation*

This step requires us to observe the outcomes of the intervention on its effectiveness. Here, we may further 'collect some data' about the changes that occur after we have introduced some intervention, and observe whether these changes are in line with our proposed hypothesis and lead to some real solution to our original problem.

2.7.3.11. *Reporting the Research*

In this step, we articulate all the activities, data collection procedures and findings that have emerged out of the research process in the form of a research report. We also ensure the presentation of the research to the wider audience.

2.8. Field Level Research

The field level research can be classified into two categories in terms of the degree of rigorousness and the procedures involved: filed experimentation, and field studies.

2.8.1. Field Experimentation

Field experimentation is a type of research study that is conducted in a real-life setting or a realistic situation by actively manipulating one and more independent variables, and by carefully controlling the influence of as many extraneous variables as the situation permits.

2.8.1.1. Limitations

i) Unlike "laboratory experiments," where we have maximum possible control, most field experiments operate with less degree of control. In simple words, the far we move from the laboratory, the more the controls we loose. Since in the field experiments, we have to come out of our laboratory and enter the field to conduct an experiment, we cannot hold our controls as tight. So, their chief limitation is regarding the control of conditions.

ii) It is practically difficult to apply the randomisation in the selection of the sample.

iii) Besides, uncontrolled environmental conditions and factors may also badly affect our dependent variables.

iv) Also, the researcher or experimenter him/herself may have certain biases that, in field experimentation, are difficult to be controlled and which influence the research process and the research findings.

Despite all these shortcomings, field experimentation is highly important for certain reasons. We should not forget that not all types of problem can be studied in the laboratory under controlled conditions. Also, even in the laboratory research, we sometimes fail to impose complete controls. Many times, there occur such problems that cannot be studied in the laboratory. We can at best study them only through field experiments. Besides, field experiments are better for studying many problems. We must not only conduct more and more field experimentation but also should do so by making all of our relevant variables operational in real-world terms. So, besides testing the theory, field experimentation provides solutions to the real-world problems.

2.8.2. Field Studies

Field studies is the ex post facto scientific inquiries aimed at discovering the relations and interactions among sociological, psychological, and educational variables in real social structures. It includes all types of scientific studies, large or small, that systematically pursue relations and test hypotheses, that are ex post facto, and that are done in real life situations like schools, communities, factories, organizations and institutions. In field studies, the researcher generally does not manipulate independent variables and studies the relations among the attitudes, perceptions, values, and behaviour of the subjects in real social or institutional situations.

2.8.2.1. *Types of field studies*

Field studies can be divided into two:

Exploratory: The exploratory type field studies seek what is. It has three main objectives: (a) to explore significant variables in the field situation, (b) to explore relations between or among the variables, and (c) to prepare the platform for systematic and rigorous hypothesis testing.

Hypothesis Testing: Just like scientific research, in field studies, hypothesis testing requires some preliminary methodological and measurement investigation, after which we retain or reject our research hypothesis.

The following are the advantages of field studies:

— The realism of field studies is strong in that these are the closest to real life and there is no complaint of artificiality in these studies.

— These are socially significant since they may lead to practical solutions of the problems.

— Also, the field studies are supported to be strong on the strength of variables, theory orientation, and heuristic quality.

Field studies suffer from the following weaknesses:

— The ex post facto character of these studies is their most serious limitation.

— We cannot precisely measure the field variables because of the greater complexity of the field situations.

— Some potential weaknesses of the subjects are sampling, feasibility, cost and time factor.

Before beginning a field study, the researcher must judge and evaluate the requirement of large amounts of time, skills, energy and money for successful completion of the field studies. It is believed that besides being a skillful investigator, the field researcher must also be a good salesman, administrator, and entrepreneur.

2.9. Conclusion

The selection of a research method is the prerogative of the researcher. He/she can select any method according to his/her wish. The subject of research determines which category a research falls under. While selecting subjects, a researcher should ensure its relevance too.

References

Campbell, D. T. and Stanley, J. C., "Experimental and quasi-experimental designs for research on teaching", In N. L. Gage (Ed.) *Handbook of Research in Teaching*, Chicago: Rand McNally and Company, 1963.

Corey, S. M., *Action Research to Improve School Practices*, New York: Teachers College, Columbia University, 1953.

Good, C. V., Barr, A. S., and Scates, D. E., *Methodology of Educational Research*, New York: Appleton-Century Crofts, Inc., 1941.

Kerlinger, F. N., *Foundations of Behavioural Research* (2nd ed.), Delhi: Surjeet Publications, 1983.

Kothari, C. R., *Research Methodology: Methods and Techniques* (2nd ed.), New Delhi: Wishwa Prakashan, 1990.

Koul, L., *Methodology of Educational Research*, New Delhi: Vikas Publishing House Pvt. Ltd., 1997.

Wallace, M. J., *Action Research for Language Teachers*, Cambridge: Cambridge University Press, 1998.

3

Research Proposal

3.1. Introduction

A research proposal is a type of blue print. It is a systematic plan, which brings to focus the preliminary planning that will be needed to accomplish the purpose of the proposed study.

3.1.1. Significance of Research Proposal

The research proposals may be of significant importance to the researcher, research supervisor and to the funding agencies.

For the Researcher: Many institutions require the researchers to submit a proposal or synopsis of the research study for approval. This blueprint serves as a guide which provides a systematic plan of steps and procedures to be followed by the researcher while conducting the research study. So, it makes it feasible and easy for the researcher to carry on the research study as per the guidelines of the research proposal. The preparation of a proper research proposal is sometimes considered as the research work half done.

For the Research Supervisor: The research proposal provides the research supervisor a basis for supervision during the period of his/her supervision. The researcher presents his/her initial draft of the research proposal before the research supervisor for critical comments and suggestions. The supervisor reviews the draft very carefully and suggests necessary modifications. If necessary, suggestions and comments may be invited from other experts of the field also. The final draft is prepared after several reviews and modifications. Later, it helps the research supervisor and serves as a basis for guiding the researcher and for reviewing the progress of the research done by the researcher.

For the Funding Agencies: Various funding agencies are the University Grants Commission (UGC), the National Council of Educational Research and Training (NCERT), the Indian Council of Social Sciences Research (ICSSR), and other national level and/ or state level agencies or institutions which provide financial assistance for conducting the research work. Almost all these agencies require the researcher to submit the research proposal or synopsis of the research study he/she wants to conduct. These agencies have a committee of experts who critically review the qualifications, research experience and research skills of the researcher, and the practical utility and feasibility of the proposed research to examine whether all perquisite conditions meet their particular respective criteria. Only after this, they may decide to provide the financial assistance.

3.1.2. Types of Research Proposal

On the basis of the type and purpose of the research study, research proposals can be broadly categorised as:

3.1.2.1. Research Proposal for Degree

This common type of proposal is prepared and presented by those researchers who are required to conduct a research study for the fulfillment of their Master's degree or Doctoral degree in education. Most universities require the beginner researchers to submit the research proposal that is then evaluated by a committee of experienced experts. These experts determine the significance, utility and feasibility of the proposed study and may suggest some modifications in the research proposal.

3.1.2.2. For Financial Support

Many times conducting a particular research seems to go beyond the budget of the researcher for which he/she requires some financial assistance. He/she then submits the research proposal to a government or private agency requesting for financial assistance. Such an agency then asks empanelled experts for comments and/or recommendations after evaluating the proposal, and the agency then decides to provide (or not to provide) the financial assistance on the basis of these comments and/or recommendations.

3.1.2.3. *For Grants by Government*

Since various research organisations such as universities, the UGC, the NCERT, and the ICSSR are earmarking more and more funds at present for a specific purpose of promoting research, more and more college and university teachers are becoming motivated to conduct research in their respective areas of concern at school, college, or university level. They are also required to submit their research proposal for evaluation and are provided grants if experts recommend so after evaluation of the research proposal.

3.2. Preparation of Research Proposal

There is no universally accepted format for preparing a research proposal. Most of the funding agencies and institutions require the researchers to submit their research proposals as per the specific formats of that agency. Before submitting a proposal for funding, it is advisable to follow the particular format that is specified by the funding agencies. However, almost all the formats ask for certain specifications of the plan to appear in the research proposal. These specifications provide sufficient information about the researcher's planning and for evaluation of the research proposal. There are certain specifications which are common to all types of research proposals and are included in all types of formats. These are:

- Statement and significance of the problem for research.
- Delimiting the boundary of the proposed study and elaborating its substantive components.
- Sources and procedure of data collection.
- Analysis of the data and policy implications.
- Time and cost estimation.
- Bio-data of the researcher.

A proper research proposal should be framed on the basis of the following guidelines:

3.2.1. Title of the Project

The title of the research proposal is just the name of the topic and suggests the theme of the work to be done. While selecting the title of the project, the researcher should take care that instead of using flowery words, professional language and terms should be used in an easy and understandable way. Also, the title should be brief, concise and specific. 'Specific' in the sense that it should claim for the study what it is going to actually deliver. So, a good title is that which provides sufficient information about the nature of the proposed project.

3.2.2. Statement of the Problem

The problem may be presented either as a declarative statement or in a question form. It serves as a goal that gives direction to the researcher. A problem, in very simple words, means that we either know nothing about a given phenomenon or there is some controversy or difference of opinion about that phenomenon. Books, journals, experts' opinions, theories, previous research, personal experiences are some of the sources from where the problems generate.

This is highly important for both the researcher and the evaluator of research proposal to focus on the significance of the problem. The researcher must show how his/her research work is going to contribute to the existing knowledge or influence the educational theory and/or practice. He/she must focus on the significance and relevance of his/her study. And, in order to maintain the quality of educational research, the evaluator must critically examine the significance and relevance of the submitted proposal. Those studies which are going to result in nothing but wastage of resources, time, money and energy must be abandoned if they don't cross the threshold of 'significance'. If we would have applied this criterion of significance rigorously, a lot of weight of untouched, unread and forgotten dissertations or theses in our libraries could had been avoided which are buried under tons of dust today.

3.2.3. Definitions, Assumptions, Limitations And Delimitations

The researcher should define all the unusual terms that others could misinterpret. The operational definitions of the variables should be given in the research proposal. These definitions establish and explain the frame of reference with which the problem is being viewed and approached.

Assumptions are those statements which are assumed to be the facts but can't be verified without testing. The researcher should give sufficient details and bases of these assumptions in his/her research proposal.

Limitations are those uncontrollable conditions which restrict the conclusions of the study and their application and generalisation to other situations. These limitations, such as inability to select the sample randomly or inability to use validated test for data collection, should be properly reported in the research proposal.

Delimitations are the limits or boundaries of our study. A project may focus on the achievement motivation in relation to the socio-economic-status of the 10th grade students. Here the conclusions can't be extended beyond this studied population.

3.2.4 Review of the Literature

While reviewing the literature you may notice some gap in knowledge or find some confusing or confiicting results and you may think of filling in this gap or to remove this confusion by conducting a research study. Since this is just a research proposal (and not a thesis or dissertation) we must describe very briefly the theoretical and empirical framework from which the problem has taken birth. Increasing the number of pages by just listing a lot of annotated studies is simply useless, ineffective and inappropriate. We must report only those studies that are highly relevant to our selected problem. Our focus must be on the latest research findings pertinent to our problem. We must emphasise the need of researching, exploring and studying this problem on the basis of existing literature. We may report here those related studies that are found in journals, books, magazines etc.

Reviewing the literature has certain advantages:

- First, this indicates that the researcher has done a lot of hard work in choosing this problem and he/she is aware with what has already been researched and also with what is to be researched.
- Second, 'review of the literature' eliminates the risk and chances of duplication of the already researched work.

— Third, it also helps the researcher in formulating the hypotheses on the basis of what is already known about that particular problem.

3.2.5. Hypothesis

Hypothesis is a tentative solution to our problem which is tested on the basis of the analysis of the collected data. In our research proposal, we should specify one major hypothesis and several minor hypotheses as the case and need may be. Hypotheses are not just guesswork, rather depend on logic and previous knowledge. These give direction to the data-gathering and research process. While formulating hypothesis we must use simplest possible terms and language instead of tough and highly technical wordings. The hypothesis should also be reasonable and consistent with previously known facts and/or theories. Also, we must state it in such a way that we can test it and find it to be either probably true or probably false.

It is just a tentative solution to the problem which can be found false also after testing. It is not a matter of worry, and this also is still a significant finding. If we are about to reject our hypothesis we must report the findings objectively instead of playing with the data to mould it as per our hypothesis. So, testing hypothesis is simply a research process or statistical process of verification or disconfirmation. Also, it is equally important that we should formulate our hypotheses before the data are actually gathered. This will lead us to scientific and unbiased investigation of our research problem.

3.2.6. Method

Here, we usually specify the nature of the subjects selected through sampling procedure, tools to be used, procedures, and data analysis techniques which we are planning to apply on the collected data.

3.2.6.1. Subjects

In this section, we provide complete information about the population from which we are planning to draw our sample. Although it depends upon our problem which we are proposing to solve, yet most frequently studied variables are the subjects' age, gender, race, caste, religion, socio-economic-status, educational level, IQ, etc. In this section, we also have to describe the size of the sample (the number of the subjects to be studied) and the sampling procedures (how the sample will be selected from the population). The research proposal is considered successful if the reader clearly understands the place and procedure of the selection of the sample.

3.2.6.2. Tools

The use of any reliable and valid tool(s) is inevitable for the collection of evidence or data for the research study. The researcher may use existing standardised test(s) or may construct his/her own as per the requirements of his/her study. If he/she has to develop a test he/she must be well versed with the test construction procedure and the standardisation process, besides being versed in using these tools.

The researcher, in the research proposal should fully describe the tool(s) to be used, the reliability and validity of the tool(s), and the reasons of the selection of that particular tool or tools for data collection. If he/she is going to develop his/her own tool, he should outline the procedure he/she is going to follow in test development and standardisation.

3.2.6.3. Procedure

Here we describe our complete future plans of the research study in detail: what we are going to do, how shall we do it, what type of the data will be required, how it will be collected, processed and analysed. There is not a single universal procedure which can be followed in all types of research studies, rather it highly depends on our particular research objectives.

3.2.6.4. Data-Analysis

Mainly, there are two types of data: qualitative and quantitative. Both the types of data are to be analysed differently. Mostly there are different types of statistical techniques to analyse these two different types of data. What particular statistical technique is to be used, and how the data are to be analysed depend on our particular study. If the data are to be processed through the computer this should also be explained in the research proposal.

We should clearly describe our complete data-analysis procedures in our research proposal so that the readers may get a clear idea of our research plan.

3.2.7. References/Bibliography

In our research proposal, we should list all the references that were cited in the text. We should cite in the research proposal the material that have helped in the preparation of the research proposal. In this case, we should prepare and present bibliography in which all the relevant references, whether cited or not, are included. It is recommendable to prepare this list alphabetically and according to the set pattern of writing the references.

3.2.8. Time Schedule

In the research proposal, the researcher should also indicate a realistic time schedule to complete the project. The study can be divided into phases and a time period can be assigned for the completion of each phase. It is very helpful for the researcher in terms of both using time systematically and minimising the natural tendency of procrastination.

Whereas the projects are to be completed in the fixed time limits, such time budgeting is highly important. With the help of this time schedule, the research supervisor may also keep an eye on the progress of research with much ease. And, above all, this schedule acts as a motivator in helping and motivating the researcher to move more confidently and systematically toward his/her ultimate goal of the completion of the research.

3.2.9. Budget Schedule

Conducting research requires a lot of money also. We should, while preparing our research proposal, estimate the cost of the project considering the required person-months and facilities. This budget along with the research proposal should be submitted to either to government, private or any other agency for their financial assistance.

In your research proposal you should justify the allocation of money for the various heads of our budget estimates because the funding agency is going to evaluate this very critically. We should prepare these estimates very carefully and under the guidance of any experienced expert. We should also consider the total time and money required, and procedure involved in conducting this research at the time of estimating the budget.

3.3. Making of Effective Research Proposal

Preparing an effective research proposal is an applied art and intelligent activity. Here are some suggestions for preparing an effective research proposal:

i) You should write the research proposal very carefully. If you write the proposal carelessly, it gives the clear message to the evaluators that the research study would also be carried out carelessly. In preparing research proposals, you should follow the format or guidelines as specified by the institution or agency where you are going to submit you proposal.

ii) The statement of the problem should be prepared in simple language and in such a way so that it should reflect significance of the problem and its contribution to the field of knowledge.

iii) You should indicate that the field of investigation is not unfamiliar and bizarre to you and you have gone through the recent trends and findings of your problem area thoroughly.

iv) The statement of hypotheses should be in correct form clearly indicating the basis for these hypotheses.

v) Provide each and every detail of your proposed procedure.

vi) You should describe in proper way your sampling procedures, the tools you are going to use, the rationale behind their use, their reliability and validity, etc.

vii) You should identify and make a list of extraneous variables that might have negative impact on your study and indicate how you are going to control them and/or minimise their effect.

viii) Clearly indicate, with rationale, which statistical techniques you are going to apply to your data.

ix) Present your budget estimate in a proper manner with clear rationale of approximate expenditure on various heads.

x) In your bio-data, present an impressive (but not exaggerated) image of yourself and show your competence to take over and complete this project objectively and successfully.

If you want to learn the research process the only best approach is to "learn by doing". Unless you begin and do it, you can't understand the research process sitting idle.

3.4. Preparing Bio-data of Researcher

Your funding agency or any other institution, where you are going to submit your research proposal for financial assistance, evaluates not only your proposal but also your qualifications, research experience and skills, and your competency of completing this research project satisfactorily. Here, you should provide some tangible proof of your research competence and capabilities. You may do so by presenting your academic qualifications and training, the list of research projects that you have completed successfully (whether independently or jointly), and your published scholarly research work, including articles and abstracts of your research studies. If your agency or institution has specified any bio-data format you must follow that.

3.5. Procedures of Conducting a Research

Generally, all research in education follow the following seven broad steps that are similar to the steps followed in the scientific method. Here is a brief overview of the research process given in these seven steps:

3.5.1. Finding Research Problem

Sometimes we experience that there is something we don't know and we want to know or explore that unknown. In research terminology, this is known as a 'problem.' The research process begins with the identification and formulation of a research problem.

3.5.2. Review of the Literature

Once we have formulated or selected a research problem, we dive into the ocean of literature to find out whether the problem has already been researched or what the related literature reveals about it.

3.5.3. Formulation of Hypothesis

On the basis of the reviewed literature, from where we selected the latest and significant findings pertinent to our problem, we formulate some hypotheses that serve as a guide also during the research process.

3.5.4. Method or Research Methodology

After we have selected a problem and formulated a working hypothesis for research, we prepare our research plan to solve this problem and to test our hypothesis. Here, we specify our research design, sample, and tools that we require to study our problem.

3.5.5. Data Collection

After selecting the sample as per the sampling procedures and the tools that are required as per the needs of our study, we start collecting the data.

3.5.6. Analysis and Interpretation of the data/results

Once we obtained the desired information, our next step is to organise the data logically, into tables and figures so that these may be analysed statistically. Then we interpret our findings in terms of the existing knowledge and in the light of our hypotheses. Here we try to explain what actually our data mean.

3.5.7. Reporting the Results

The last step of the research process is to report your findings and get them published somewhere (or get widely circulated) so that people may get benefit of your conclusions and/or may draw some ideas for further research. After acquainting ourselves with the research process in brief, let us now turn to the minute details.

3.6. Conclusion

Research is a very serious process and the procedures of this must be follow carefully and responsibly. From the conceptualisation and till its completion, the researcher should be aware of the seriousness of the work that he/she is going to undertake. A research is a series of process. It is like the anthesis of a flower. A careless work will belittle the entire process.

References

Christensen, L. B., *Experimental Methodology* (6th ed.), Boston: Allyn and Bacon, 1994.

Kerlinger, F. N., *Foundations of Behavioural Research*, Delhi: Surjeet Publications, 1973.

Kothari, C. R., *Research Methodology: Methods and Techniques (2nd ed.)*, New Delhi: Wishwa Prakashan, 1990.

Koul, L., *Methodology of Educational Research*, New Delhi: Vikas Publishing House Pvt. Ltd., 1997.

Marx, M. H., *Theories in Contemporary Psychology*, New York: Macmillan, 1963.

Nachmias, D. and Nachmias, C., *Research Methods in the Social Sciences*, New York: St. Martin's Press, 1981.

4

Formulation of Hypothesis

4.1. Introduction

A hypothesis is a logical supposition, a reasonable guess, an educated conjecture. It provides a tentative explanation for a phenomenon under investigation. However, hypotheses are not unique to research. Hypotheses are constantly generated in the human mind as we work to understand day-to-day phenomena. By formulating a series of reasonable guesses of cause and effect we are able to understand and explore the events in our surrounding environment.

A hypothesis is important because it guides the research. An investigator may refer to the hypothesis to direct his or her thought process toward the solution of the research problem or sub-problems. The hypothesis helps an investigator to collect the right kinds of data needed for the investigation. Hypotheses are also important because they help an investigator to locate information needed to resolve the research problem or sub-problems.

In research, an investigator is able to either support or reject a hypothesis. If a hypothesis is rejected, it will lead an investigator to new hypothesis to explain the phenomenon in question. If a hypothesis is continually supported, it may evolve into a theory.

As a hypothesis is continually supported over time by a growing body of data, it becomes a theory. A theory is describes as "an organised body of concepts and principles intended to explain a particular phenomenon." A theory is similar to a hypothesis in that it offers a tentative explanation for a phenomenon that new data will either support or not support. Both are supported or rejected based on testing by various investigators under different conditions.

A theory that is continually validated over time by a growing body of data becomes a law. Often times, an investigator will formulate a hypothesis based on the problem or sub-problems of the research. The hypothesis is driven by the research question.

4.2. Formulation of Research Hypothesis

Research hypotheses are the specific testable predictions made about the independent and dependent variables in the study. Usually the literature review has given background material that justifies the particular hypotheses that are to be tested. Hypotheses are couched in terms of the particular independent and dependent variables that are going to be used in the study.

A hypothesis is a tentative explanation for certain behaviours, phenomena, or events that have occurred or will occur.

— The hypothesis states the researcher's expectations concerning the relationship between the variables in the research problem.

— It is a refinement of the research problem. It is the most specific statement of the problem.

— It states what the researcher thinks the outcome of the study will be.

— The researcher collects data that either supports the hypothesis or does not support it.

— The hypothesis is formulated following the review of related literature and prior to the execution of the study. The related literature leads the researcher to expect a certain relationship.

— A good hypothesis states as clearly and concisely as possible the expected relationship (or differences) between two variables and defines those variables in operational, measurable terms.

— A well-stated and defined hypothesis must be and will be if well-formulated and stated) testable. It should be possible to support or not support the hypothesis by collecting and analysing data.

A hypothesis differs from a problem. A problem is formulated in the form of a question; it serves as the basis or origin from which an hypothesis is derived. A hypothesis is a suggested solution to a problem. A problem (question) cannot be directly tested, whereas a hypothesis can be tested and verified.

A hypothesis is formulated after the problem has been stated and the literature study has been concluded. It is formulated when the researcher is totally aware of the theoretical and empirical background to the problem.

4.2.1. Function of a Hypothesis

A hypothesis offers explanations for the relationships between those variables that can be empirically tested. It furnishes proof that the researcher has sufficient background knowledge to enable him/her to make suggestions in order to extend existing knowledge. It gives direction to an investigation and structures the next phase in the investigation and therefore furnishes continuity to the examination of the problem.

4.2.2. Characteristics of a Hypothesis

A hypothesis should have elucidating power and should strive to furnish an acceptable explanation of the phenomenon. It must be verifiable and be formulated in simple, understandable terms. Besides, it should corresponds with existing knowledge.

4.2.3. Classification of Hypothesis

Hypotheses can be classified in terms of their derivation (inductive and deductive hypotheses) and in terms of their formulation (research—directional and non-directional and statistical or null hypotheses).

4.2.3.1. Research Hypothesis

It is a relationship between variables and indicates the nature of the relationship. Here, if A is valid, B follows ...

E.g.: "If you hit a child with a cain, he/she will cry.

4.2.3.2. Null Hypothesis

Hypotheses are simply if-then sentences that can be categorised in certain logical forms, such as no difference (null hypothesis), associated difference, directionality of difference, and magnitude of difference. A good hypothesis implies all these in a single sentence, and the trick is to express them as briefly as possible and in simple English.

The null hypothesis remains unstated or implied as no differences, no matter how complex your other (called alternative) hypotheses get. Technically, all statistical tests are tests of the null hypothesis first, which is rejected in favour of degrees of confidence in the alternatives.

4.2.3.3 Statistical Hypotheses

The statistical hypotheses consist of the null hypothesis (H_0) and the alternative hypothesis (H_1). In other words the null hypothesis states that there is no difference between the two means on the reading comprehension test scores, while the alternative hypothesis states that the girls mean score on the reading comprehension test will significantly exceed that of the boys. Generally we use a statistical test (e.g. the t-test) to decide if the girls score significantly higher than the boys.

4.2.4. Method of Writing Hypotheses

Most students believe that they are going to be experimenting anytime they are given a laboratory assignment in science. However, more often than not, students are doing something other than experiments. This is not necessarily bad. A good deal of science is observational and descriptive. For example, the study of bio-diversity usually involves looking at wide variety of specimens and maybe sketching and recording their unique characteristics. However, there are other times when we science teachers are trying to teach students how scientists work and how we can verify things which others may say or believe is so without any proof.

To learn about what is not known or to verify a notion, the so-called "scientific method" might be carried out and an actual experiment may be conducted. It does not matter that your experiment has been done a thousand times before or that your teacher already knows the results. What matters is that you don't know the results and that you can independently find a verifiable answer. In real experiments, real hypotheses should be written before the actual experiment.

4.2.5. Real Hypothesis

A useful hypothesis is a testable statement which may include a prediction. A hypotheses should not be confused with a theory. Theories are general explanations based on a large amount of data. For example, the theory of evolution applies to all living things and is based on wide range of observations. However, there are many things about evolution that are not fully understood such as gaps in the fossil record. Many hypotheses have been proposed and tested.

4.2.6. Formatting Hypotheses

Most commonly, hypotheses take three formats:

i) a question, "Does temperature affect fermentation?"

ii) a conditional statement, "Temperature may affect fermentation."

iii) an If, then statement, "If fermentation rate is related to temperature, then increasing the temperature will increase gas production".

The third type is more structured and so it is a "formalised" hypothesis. The structure of a formalised hypothesis is useful because it makes the student focus on two variables that may be related. Furthermore, it forces the student to make a prediction of how manipulating one variable independent will affect the other variable dependent.

In the formalised hypotheses the "if" clause proposes a relationship between two things, the variables. The variables here are diffusion rate and molecular size. In the experimental design, we can manipulate molecular size by simply selecting soluble substances of different molecular size, e.g., iodine, glucose, starch. The student will know what the dependent variable is because it is the thing she/he watches for results, i.e. movement of iodine (colour), glucose (indicator change), and starch (indicator change).

If this hypothesis is stated as a question (Does molecular size affect diffusion through a membrane?) the student must infer what is to be manipulated and what is to be observed. Furthermore, the student doesn't have to make a prediction. Experience has taught me that few students infer what relationship is implied by a hypothesis in the question format. Another value of a formalised hypothesis is that when a student is given such a hypothesis, he can be asked to design an experiment that will test the hypothesis.

4.3. Hypothesis and Variables

A variable is a concept or construct that can vary or have more than one value. Some variables can be quite concrete such as gender, birth order, weight, or shoe size. Others can be considerably more abstract, vague, and squishy. For example, sense of well being, self-esteem, strength of belief in religion, or IQ. Basically, variables are the things about people that we can say one person has more of than another. So we find that people vary in their gender and shoe size, and their self-esteem and their IQ.

We might then be interested in knowing how certain variables are related to each other. For example, which variables predict self-esteem (itself, another variable). We might be interested in understanding the relationship between self-esteem and variables such as whether or not the person is employed, his or her depression level, the persons sex, and the number of failed relationships the person has had.

There are two basic kinds of variables. The independent variable is defined as the "variable that the experimenter manipulates." While this is true in experiments, not all studies are experiments. Independent variable could imply that there is no independent variable in correlational studies.

The independent variable is what we are studying with respect to how it is related to or influences the dependent variable. If the independent variable is related to or influences the dependent variable, it can be used to predict the dependent variable. It is therefore sometimes called the predictor variable, or the explanatory variable. The independent variable may be manipulated or it may just be measured. In contrast, the dependent variable is what we are studying, with respect to how it is related to or influenced by the independent variable or how it can be explained or predicted by the independent variable.

The independent variable is the kind of advice the parents give and the dependent variable is whether the child has criminal

record or not. A useful hint for determining which variable is which in a study is to ask whether you are trying to either influence or predict one variable from some other variable or variables. If so, that variable is probably the dependent variable. The variable that you are using to make the predictions or to determine if it influences (rather than is influenced by) some other variable in the study is typically the independent variable. For this reason, the independent variable is sometimes called the "explanatory" variable while the dependent variable is sometimes called the "response" variable. You try to "explain" variation in responses on the dependent variable with the independent or "explanatory" variable(s).

The building blocks of hypotheses are variables. A variable is anything that varies, changes, or has differences. Something that never changes is called a constant. Variables that only have two extremes are called attributes. In social science research, we deal mostly with two types of variables: independent and dependent. Independent variables are those things thought to be the cause or bring about change in other variables. Dependent variables are those things changed or affected by independent variables, sometimes through other variables. Independent variables always come before dependent variables in time and space.

An important part of the research process that goes along with hypothesis formulation is constructing your operational definitions. These are definitions of your variables for research purposes. They are important so others can understand and replicate your research. Researchers need to define their variables very precisely, especially the dependent variables.

4.3.1. Types of Variables

A variable is a measurable characteristic that varies. It may change from group to group, person to person, or even within one person over time. There are six common variable types:

4.3.1.1. Dependent Variables

It shows the effect of manipulating or introducing the independent variables. For example, if the independent variable is the use or non-use of a new language teaching procedure, then the dependent variable might be students' scores on a test of the content taught using that procedure. In other words, the variation in the dependent variable depends on the variation in the independent variable.

4.3.1.2. Independent Variables

These are those that the researcher has control over. This "control" may involve manipulating existing variables (e.g., modifying existing methods of instruction) or introducing new variables in the research setting. Whatever the case may be, the researcher expects that the independent variable(s) will have some effect on (or relationship with) the dependent variables.

4.3.1.3. Intervening Variables

It refers to abstract processes that are not directly observable but that link the independent and dependent variables. In language learning and teaching, they are usually inside the subjects' heads, including various language learning processes which the researcher cannot observe. For example, if the use of a particular teaching technique is the independent variable and mastery of the objectives is the dependent variable, then the language learning processes used by the subjects are the intervening variables.

4.3.1.4. Moderator Variables

It affects the relationship between the independent and dependent variables by modifying the effect of the intervening variable(s). Unlike extraneous variables, moderator variables are measured and taken into consideration. Typical moderator variables in TESL and language acquisition research (when they are not the major focus of the study) include the sex, age, culture, or language proficiency of the subjects.

4.3.1.5. Control Variables

Language learning and teaching are very complex processes. It is not possible to consider every variable in a single study. Therefore, the variables that are not measured in a particular study must be held constant, neutralised/balanced, or eliminated, so they will not have a biasing effect on the other variables. Variables that have been controlled in this way are called control variables.

4.3.1.6. *Extraneous Variables*

These are those factors in the research environment which may have an effect on the dependent variable(s) but which are not controlled. Extraneous variables are dangerous. They may damage a study's validity, making it impossible to know whether the effects were caused by the independent and moderator variables or some extraneous factor. If they cannot be controlled, extraneous variables must at least be taken into consideration when interpreting results.

4.4. Hypothesis Testing

An essential component of the scientific process is the formulation and evaluation of hypotheses. In seeking to learn more about the social world, social scientists ask many different kinds of questions about relationships between factors of social life. How do investors change their behaviour when market conditions change? What role did political and social factors play in the Salem witch trials? Do feelings of connectedness influence students' performance in school? To address these questions, social scientists form hypotheses which they then evaluate using some form of data.

You may be familiar with examples of hypotheses and hypothesis testing from the natural sciences, perhaps through schoolwork or participation in a school science fair. Typically, hypotheses are generated from some theory or theoretical perspective, then evaluated using data collected through some laboratory procedures.

In examining phenomena of the social world, there are any number of relationships that we could examine to learn more about their workings. However, it is possible that some of the relationships that we observe might be due to chance, rather than some relationship between two variables.

4.4.1. Preparing Hypotheses

In social science research, we establish two competing hypotheses that we then evaluate in light of some empirical data. These hypotheses are referred to as the null hypothesis and the alternative hypothesis. The primary purpose of hypothesis t[illegible] is to examine the likelihood of the null hypothesis wi[illegible]

The null hypothesis is often the reverse of what the experimenter actually believes; it is put forward to allow the data to contradict it. In the study of the effect of sense of control on health, the researchers expect that a sense of control will improve health. The null hypothesis they would establish in this setting, then, is that enhancing sense of control will have no effect on health. The alternative hypothesis is one that stands in contrast to the null, usually that the condition or change will have some effect. In the sense of control example, the alternative hypothesis is that changes in sense of control will result in a change in health.

Depending on the data, the null hypothesis either will or will not be rejected as a viable possibility. If the data show a sufficiently large effect of the sense of control, then the null hypothesis that sense of control has no effect can be rejected. Specific criteria used to accept or reject the null hypothesis are discussed in the modules describing statistical tests used to evaluate hypotheses. With this understanding of the way that hypotheses are generated in the social sciences, you're ready to look at specific tools that are used to test hypotheses.

4.5. Conclusion

Formulation of hypothesis is one of the most important parts of a research. A wrong hypothesis and its testing leads a researcher only in a wrong direction. The hypothesis must be good enough to lead a researcher in the right path.

References

Gillespie, M., "Research Within Reach", *Focus on Basics* 2, Spring, 1989.

Goetz, J. and LeCompte, M., *Ethnography and Qualitative Design in Educational Research*, London: Academic Press, 1984.

Gordon Wells (Editor), *Action, Talk, and Text: Learning and Teaching Through Inquiry*, Practitioner InquiryTeachers College Press, 2000.

5

Research Problems

A research problem is the situation that causes the researcher to feel apprehensive, confused and ill at ease. It is the demarcation of a problem area within a certain context involving the Who or What, the Where, the When and the Why of the problem situation.

There are many problem situations that may give rise to research. Three sources usually contribute to problem identification. Own experience or the experience of others may be a source of problem supply. A second source could be scientific literature. You may read about certain findings and notice that a certain field was not covered. This could lead to a research problem. Theories could be a third source. Shortcomings in theories could be researched.

Research can thus be aimed at clarifying or substantiating an existing theory, at clarifying contradictory findings, at correcting a faulty methodology, at correcting the inadequate or unsuitable use of statistical techniques, at reconciling conflicting opinions, or at solving existing practical problems.

5.1. Detection of the Problem

Research originates from a need that arises. A clear distinction between the PROBLEM and the PURPOSE should be made. The problem is the aspect the researcher worries about, thinks about, wants to find a solution for. The purpose is to solve the problem, ie find answers to the question(s). If there is no clear problem formulation, the purpose and methods are meaningless. While formulating a problem, the following should be keep in mind:

i) Outline the general context of the problem area.
ii) Highlight key theories, concepts and ideas current in this area.

iii) What appear to be some of the underlying assumptions of this area?

iv) Why are these issues identified important?

v) What needs to be solved?

vi) Read round the area (subject) to get to know the background and to identify unanswered questions or controversies, and/or to identify the most significant issues for further exploration.

The research problem should be stated in such a way that it would lead to analytical thinking on the part of the researcher with the aim of possible concluding solutions to the stated problem. Research problems can be stated in the form of either questions or statements.

The research problem should always be formulated grammatically correct and as completely as possible. Avoid meaningless words. Demarcate the research field into manageable parts by dividing the main problem into sub-problems is of the utmost importance.

5.1.1. Sub-problem(s)

Sub-problems are problems related to the main problem identified. Sub-problems flow from the main problem and make up the main problem. It is the means to reach the set goal in a manageable way and contribute to solving the problem.

5.1.2. Statement of the Problem

The statement of the problem involves the demarcation and formulation of the problem, ie the Who/What, Where, When, Why. It usually includes the statement of the hypothesis.

5.2. Types of Research Problems

One long-honoured tradition in academia is that of professors assigning thesis and dissertation topics to their advisees instead of having students create topics of their own. Or, if faculty supervisors don't actually assign topics, they may at least suggest what their advisees might study. There are both advantages and disadvantages to assigned research problems. Perhaps the most obvious advantage of adopting a professor's proposal is that you ensure that your mentor enthusiastically endorses your project.

Assigned topics are often part of a faculty member's own research programme, with each student's topic representing one piece of a complex puzzle the professor is trying to solve. And if the research is funded by a grant, you may get paid for working on the portion that involves your thesis or dissertation. If a report of the research is published in a journal or in conference proceedings, you may also be credited as a coauthor. Or your mentor may acknowledge your participation in a footnote to a journal article or book chapter.

Accepting a topic that is part of someone else's research not only relieves you of hunting for a research problem, but it may also lighten your burden of devising a design, creating data-gathering instruments, and interpreting the results. Those tasks may already have been performed by the professor or his staff. However, depending so heavily on others for a research problem robs you of the opportunity to work out such matters for yourself. So, from the standpoint of gaining experience generating and solving problems on your own, an assigned topic that is accompanied by assigned research procedures may get you your degree with less pain, but it may not serve as the best preparation for future research you wish to pursue on your own.

There certainly is no shortage of worthy research problems if you know how to hunt. Perhaps the best way to generate problems is to cultivate the habit of critical reading and listening. This means constantly bringing questions to mind while you are poring over books and journals and while you witness lectures and discussions. The sorts of questions you pose identify the kinds of problems to investigate. Beyond critical reading and listening, a further source of topics is that of problems met on the job, either on your own job or someone else's. In order to illustrate how such search strategies work, the following examples demonstrate specific ways of using critical reading/listening and on-the-job problems for discovering suitable topics.

5.2.1. Critical Reading and Listening

Questions you ask about what you read or hear can concern (a) the significance or focus of an author's research topic, (b) the applicability of an author's results to other populations, times, or places, (c) a researcher's methods of collecting information, (d) ways data have been classified, (e) an author's theory of what causes events to occur as they do, (f) applications of theories, or (g) some combination of several of these matters.

In all research, the information an investigator collects encompasses only a limited number of people, objects, activities, or events. Sometimes researchers are content to restrict their summaries and interpretations to only those people, institutions, and events they have directly studied. Consequently, when you read such studies, you may wonder whether conclusions reached in a given context actually hold true for other places and times than those directly investigated. You may, therefore, choose to devise a replication study, adopting the same methods of gathering information that were used in the original investigation but applying those methods to a different sampling of people, institutions, or events. In doing so, you are conducting comparative research, identifying the likenesses and differences between the results of the original study and your own.

5.2.2. Classification of Information

Each time you collect information to answer a research question, you must organise your data in a form that permits a description, analysis, and presentation of the results to your intended audience. This means you must adopt a system for classifying your information. Such systems are often referred to as typologies or taxonomies. Therefore, one way of finding a research problem can be that of substituting a scheme for classifying data that differs from the scheme used in an existing study. In effect, you produce a methodologically innovative thesis or dissertation.

5.3. Formation of Theories

A theory in its most basic form is (a) a description of components, variables, or factors and (b) a description of how those components interact to (c) produce some outcome. Thus, theories are explanatory in that they propose how and why things happen as they do. In your survey of how other scholars have diagnosed problems in your field of interest, you may be dissatisfied with the explanations they offered, so you try to think of a better way-

or at least an alternative way--to account for what occurred. In other words, you create a theory of your own or perhaps a variation of someone else's model. As a result, your thesis or dissertation takes the form of an explication, and perhaps an application, of your theory.

5.3.1. Risk Theory

The word risk means the likelihood that undesirable consequences will result from an action. The term educational risk estimate refers to people's expectation that they will suffer some sort of loss if they accept a role in an educational development project. Positive potential is the opposite of risk. Positive potential refers to the likelihood that people will experience personally desirable con- sequences from their participation in an educational reform. The amount of effort they will exert, either to support or to defeat an innovation, is determined by the relationship between the amount of risk and amount of positive potential they expect. Thus, a person's effort can be computed by the formula E=p-r. In other words, positive potential minus risk equals the effort an individual will expend.

A researcher's task in developing his/her dissertation consists of (a) proposing variables or conditions that influence people's perception of risks and of positive potentials, (b) defending those variables with logical analysis and empirical evidence, and (c) explaining how such variables interact to determine (d) the amount of effort individuals expend to support or to thwart an intended educational change.

5.3.2. Theory of Intelligence

Intelligence is not a singular, unified personal power which operates with equal effectiveness in all aspects of life. Instead, it is more accurately conceived to be seven separate types of ability or intelligences that make their separate contributions to the adequacy of people's performance in life's endeavours. The seven focus on (1) use of language, (2) logical-mathematical analysis, (3) spatial representation, (4) musical thinking, (5) the use of the body to solve problems or to make things, (6) an understanding of other individuals (a form of social intelligence), and (7) an understanding of oneself.

5.3.3. Social-exchange Theory

According to social-exchange theory, an individual who benefits from another person's acts is obligated to reciprocate by furnishing benefits to that person in turn. For many common types of social interaction, proper exchange is dictated by cultural tradition in the form of expectations about fairness, expectations that assume the form of exchange norms. Such norms are adopted in a culture as devices for coercing the parties in a social transaction to abide by what is considered fair. Members of society impose social pressure to encourage people to comply with those norms. The extent to which people abide by exchange norms influences their status in the society's hierarchy of respect, prestige, and power.

5.3.4. Theory of Historical Revisionism

This theory is founded on the proposition that whenever a radical change of political power occurs, the newly installed leaders seek to revise historical records in order to legitimatise their right to govern and to cast their organisation and efforts in a highly favourable light.

5.3.5. Site-based Management Theory

A graduate student in the field of administration has become especially interested in the presently popular leadership theory that organisations should be flattened, shared decision making should be adopted, and power should be decentralised. The student has informally observed several organisations in which such site-based-management (SGM) theory has been applied; and she recognises that, instead of reducing the power of the officially appointed head of the organization, the plan gives the head even more power.

5.4. Selection of a Good Topic

Nine criteria are the best method for judging the desirability of research problems. The nine standards can be cast in the form of questions about your supervising committee, "true" research, the expected outcomes of your study, the feasibility of your methods, time constraints, skills and knowledge, equipment, personnel, and funding.

5.4.1. Committee Approval

When you submit your proposal to your major advisor and other committee members, it's not sufficient to give them only a title or a question that your project is intended to answer. In addition, you need to offer a rationale telling why your problem is a good one and what methods you plan to use for gathering and analysing your data. This synopsis furnishes the information the professors need to judge your proposal. If any of your committee members consider your proposal unacceptable, you either need to change your problem or need to replace dissenting committee members with ones who approve of your topic.

The following standards are among those that faculty members typically include in judging the worth of thesis and dissertation topics.

5.4.1.2. *True Research*

Faculty members often differ in their worldviews. For instance, positivists and postmodernists can disagree vehemently over what constitutes suitable research topics and methods of investigation. Therefore, it is important that your definition of research coincides with that of the faculty members who supervise and evaluate your work.

Furthermore, students' intentions, as reflected in how they phrase their project proposals, can suggest that they are not seeking an answer to a significant question but, rather, are trying to get readers to accept a belief that those students already cherish and wish to propagate. Therefore, if you know at the outset exactly what conclusions will be drawn at the end of your project, then the project qualifies as propagandising or salesmanship rather than research.

5.4.1.3. *Significance of Outcome*

A topic that you select may qualify as research, yet still not be considered a suitable thesis or dissertation problem. One reason is that the task you pose for yourself may be too simple, in that it fails to represent the complexity and level of expertise expected of a person who deserves a graduate degree.

A second reason is that the answer you hope to derive from your investigation appears to be insignificant. While presenting your topic originally, you are obliged to indicate for whom-and why-an answer to your research question is important.

5.5. Feasible Methodology

5.5.1. Time Constraint

In the dim past, some graduate school wag created the ABD academic degree (All-But-Dissertation) which might be awarded to that large corps of doctoral candidates who completed all the course work but never finished their dissertations. Consequently, faculty advisers are often concerned about how well students' research projects fit within the time constraints imposed by (a) the college or university (some schools set a limit of five years for completing a master's programme and seven years for completing a doctorate) and (b) other time-consuming responsibilities in students' lives (a job, a family). Therefore, in presenting your project proposal to your advisors, you might profitably include a schedule of the phases that the project will involve and an estimate of the time required to complete each phase.

5.5.2. Knowledge and Skills

Doing a thesis or dissertation is a valuable learning experience, in that students are not expected at the outset to command all of the knowledge and skills required for completing their project. They gain that knowledge and skill as the project evolves. Thus, when you present your proposal to faculty members, you should be prepared to explain which knowledge and skills you already possess and which you will need to acquire. Sometimes it's not feasible for you to learn every specialised skill you need, such as complex computer programming or a foreign language, so you must depend on others for such services. Hence, it is well to estimate ahead of time what those services will be and where you intend to find them.

5.5.3. Equipment and Supplies

Although a description of needed equipment and supplies is usually not included in the written project submission, it is useful

to have that information in mind in case it is asked for by a professor who reviews your proposal.

5.5.3.1 *Personnel*

Sometimes the student who creates the project will be the sole participant in the research and perform all the necessary tasks alone. But other projects require outside help--people to serve as interviewers, test correctors, statistical analysts, and more. Because faculty committee members may inquire about the personnel who will be involved in your research, you may wish to be prepared ahead of time to answer questions about whatever assistants you will need.

5.5.3.2 *Funds*

Your principal advisor or other members of your supervising committee may ask how much your project is expected to cost and where the money will come from. In some instances they will ask only for a likely total amount. In others they will ask for a list of activities and equipment, along with an estimated cost of each. Even if your professors do not require a written expense projection, it is well to have in mind an estimated cost and source of funds.

When you submit your research proposal to your advisors, you will typically be expected to furnish a written synopsis that defines the research problem or issue, suggests why it's important to study, and explains the methods you intend to use for resolving the problem or question. Members of supervising committees may also ask about your the time period within which you expect to complete your project and the sources of the needed knowledge, skill, equipment, supplies, personnel and funds required in your plan. Whether or not you include these additional matters in your written proposal, it's well to have answers to such queries in hand when your plan is being inspected.

5.6. CONCLUSION

Research is a process of searching unknowns again and again. Research problem is just a tip of the ice berg. But while selecting a research topic, it must be worth searching. Otherwise, the whole research work will become meaningless. The problem should be relevant, and it must generate curiosity to others to know more about the topic. The success and failure of a research work also depends on the selection of a research topic. So, take care while selecting a topic.

References

Cohen, L., and Manion, I., *Research Methods in Education*, Routledge, 1989.

Campbell, A., *Practitioner research and professional development in Education*, London: Paul Chapman, 2004.

Dadds, M. and Hart, S. (Eds), *Doing Practitioner Research Differently*, Routledge Falmer, 2001.

Freeman, *Doing Teacher –Research: From Inquiry to Understanding*, Boston, Heinle and Heinle, 1998.

Hammersley, M., *Educational Research: Policymaking and Practice*, London, Paul Chapman Publishing, 2002.

Middlewood, David, Coleman, M. and Lumby, J., *Practitioner Research in Education: Making a Difference*, Paul Chapman, 1999.

6

Literature Review

6.1. Introduction

Literature review is a summary of a subject field that supports the identification of specific research questions. It needs to draw on and evaluate a range of different types of sources including academic and professional journal articles, books, and web-based resources. The literature search helps in the identification and location of relevant documents and other sources. Search engines can be used to search web resources and bibliographic databases. Conceptual frameworks can be a useful tool in developing an understanding of a subject area. Creating the literature review involves the stages such as scanning, making notes, structuring the literature review, writing the literature review, and building a bibliography.

All research needs to be informed by existing knowledge in a subject area. The literature review identifies and organises the concepts in relevant literature. When students embark on a dissertation they are typically expected to undertake a literature review at an early stage in the development of their research. Often this may be their first significant encounter with the journal and other literature on their subject. They may have successfully completed much of their undergraduate studies by relying on textbooks and lectures. One of the most intimidating aspects of a literature review is encountering the messy nature of knowledge. Concepts transcend disciplinary boundaries, and literature can be found in a wide range of different kinds of sources.

6.2. Nature of Literature Review

Literature review distills the existing literature in a subject field;

the objective of the literature review is to summarise the state of the art in that subject field. From this review of earlier and recent work, it becomes possible to identify areas in which further research would be beneficial. Indeed, the concluding paragraphs of the literature review should lead seamlessly to research propositions and methodologies. It is therefore important that the literature review is focused, and avoids the more comprehensive textbook-like approach.

Literature reviews are important in:

— supporting the identification of a research topic, question or hypothesis;
— identifying the literature to which the research will make a contribution, and contextualising the research within that literature;
— building an understanding of theoretical concepts and terminology;
— facilitating the building of a bibliography or list of the sources that have been consulted;
— suggesting research methods that might be useful; and
— in analysing and interpreting results.

6.3. Evaluation of Information Resources

A range of information sources might be used to inform the research question and design. The evaluation of these sources is a very real problem. Typically in professional disciplines, like information systems, and business and management, there will be both academic and professional literature. Both may have a role in the identification of a research theme, but the academic literature contains a firmer theoretical basis, with more critical treatment of concepts and models. Articles in scholarly and research journals should form the core of the literature review. Most such articles will be written by researchers. They will include a literature review, a discussion of the research methodology, an analysis of results, and focused statements of conclusions and recommendations. These articles are designed to record and distill systematically researched knowledge in the area, and have typically been peer refereed prior to acceptance for publication. Scholarly and research journals may also include review articles

that provide a review of all of the recent work in an area. Such reviews will include a significant bibliography that may be an invaluable source of reference to other work in the area, even if the review does not match a proposed research topic precisely.

Professional and practitioner journal articles are often around three pages in length, they may be useful in identifying recent developments or topical themes in context, policy, legal frameworks, and technological advances, but should be carefully differentiated from research and scholarly articles.

Another source that needs to be used intelligently is books. Standard texts are a good place to start. They provide a summary of current ideas and in disciplines such as business and management and information systems many are regularly updated. Books include bibliographies or lists of references to other useful sources.

Web resources are easy to locate through simple searches in standard search engines. The web provides access to a wide range of information, but these sources are provided by a range of different individuals and organisations, each with their own messages to communicate, and reasons for making the information available. It can be difficult to evaluate web resources. Many may be more suitable for the data gathering element of a research project, rather than as input to a literature review.

4.3.1. Identification of Documents

There are a number of different tools to assist in the identification and location of documents. These include:

i) *Library catalogues*—good for locating books held by a library, and journals to which they subscribe;

ii) *Search engines*—good for locating web pages, with simple keyword based searches; and,

ii) *On-line databases or abstracting and indexing services*, which provide access to journal articles, papers in conference proceedings, reports, dissertations and other documents.

While search engines make for beguilingly easy location of web pages, academic journal articles are more difficult to locate. The process often has a number of stages, and is less than obvious. To add to the complexity each route to the full text of a document is different.

Most search engines, whether they search online databases, or the web, have two levels of search options. It is possible to conduct Basic searches using keywords, or to choose the Advanced search option that offers a range of other search devices to assist in the formulation of a more precise search.

As the search algorithms that search engines use to retrieve documents have improved in recent years, it is possible to go a long way with a basic keyword search. These searches are most effective if you use a very precise term (e.g. celebrity endorsement, competitive advantage) or a name (e.g. Consignia, Amazon). The search engine will generate a list of references to web resources in a ranked order that is based on the frequency of, and location of occurrence of the words in the search term. Clicking on one of these web resources will display the appropriate web page. Often links through to related web pages will also be offered in the list of references.

Basic searches work on the terms in the search statement, and prioritise documents in which these words appear close to one another. There are numerous topics for which such a search will not necessarily provide a very focused list of references. A search on most towns names will generate entries on more than one location. Similarly searches on more specific topics, such as 'the use of information systems in human resource departments in hospitals' might benefit from more structure in the design of the search statement than is available with basic search.

Such searches benefit from the use of the advanced search option, which typically allows the searcher to be specific about the combination of words in the search statement (by using the Boolean operators, NOT, AND and OR). This option may also allow truncation of the words in the search statement, and specification of the location of the search terms in the document. The exact form of Advanced search facilities vary between the search engines used to locate web resources and those used to search bibliographic databases. Advice and guidance is usually available on the search engine help systems. There are number of different ways of going about gathering information, and developing a search strategy.

6.4. Concept Mapping

Concept map is a picture of the territory under study, and represents the concepts in that area and the relationships between them. Concepts are typically represented by labeled circles or boxes, and relationships are represented by lines or arrows.

Concept mapping is a useful way of identifying key concepts in a collection of documents or a research area. Such a map can be used to:

i) Identify additional search terms during the literature search

ii) Clarify thinking about the structure of the literature review in preparation for writing the review

ii) Understand theory, concepts and the relationships between them.

Concept maps may be sketched on paper or on a computer. It is important to recognise that there is no correct answer for a concept map—their purpose is to assist the researcher to develop their understanding. Loosely structured maps appeal to some researchers, whilst others prefer more structured approaches based on principles such as flowcharts, or hierarchies. Since concept maps are based on the researcher's understanding at the point in time when they were drafted it is likely that as the research advances they will change, with concepts being merged, or new concepts and relationships being added.

6.5. Creation of Literature Review

There are five steps in the creation of a literature review: scanning documents, making notes, and structuring the literature review, writing the literature review, and building the bibliography.

6.5.1. Scanning Documents

It provides a familiarity with the broad spectrum of documents, and the grouping of documents with similar themes. Scanning documents may give some insights into to key themes that need to be included in the literature review.

6.5.2. Making Notes

This leads to a distillation of key themes and messages. Remember to note the sources of ideas, so that the sources can be cited later. An easy way of making notes is to annotate and mark up the document, so that key pieces of text and figures an be readily located later. Resist the urge to use a marker pen on too many large chunks of text—this is really not very helpful, because it avoids the distillation and categorisation that is necessary before an integrated literature review takes shape.

6.5.3. Structuring the Literature Review

It is concerned with identifying the key themes in the review and starting to organise concepts and documents in accordance with the key themes. The structure must emerge from the literature; there is no one answer.

6.5.4. Writing the Literature Review

This can commence once a broad structure has been resolved. The headings in the structure can be used to analyse existing documents by making margin comments referring to section of the literature review. Then all of the documents with content relevant to a specific section of the literature review can be gathered together, and the writing of sections of the literature review can commence. The literature review should integrate in a coherent account three different types of material:

i) A distillation and understanding of key concepts
ii) Quotations, the words of the original writer. These should be used sparingly and for special impact. When they are used it is important to cite the author, date and page number of the quote, and to include the full reference for the source in the bibliography.
iii) A distillation of positions, research findings or theories from other authors, but written in your words. These concepts should be acknowledged with a citation.

6.5.5. Building Bibliography

A bibliography is a list of all of the sources that you have referred to in the literature review (or at other points in your dissertation).

As work progresses it is important to make a note of the documents and other sources that have been read, and, later to translate this bibliography into a list of relevant documents. Most universities specify the type of referencing system to be used and the format of citation to be adopted for different types of documents. There are two main referencing systems. One of these inserts numbers in the text, and then lists references according to numerical sequence of application in the text, at the end of the document. The other system cites documents by author name and date in the text, and arranges the list of references (or bibliography) in order according to the alphabetical sequence of the authors' names. Components of the citations listed at the end of the dissertation vary for different kinds of documents, but there are some very precise specifications as to what to include, and how to punctuate such references. A good dissertation adheres to these guidelines. The most important thing to remember about citations is that there should be sufficient data included to uniquely define a document, and to make it possible to locate it. For example, for books, edition statements and date of publication are important, and with journal articles it is important to include page numbers.

6.6. Importance of Literature Review

The purpose of a literature review is not simply to describe or summarise the literature in the field. That would be an annotated bibliography. The literature review is an active process of construction. It involves defining and problematising the field within which you will situate your own research. A literature review involves providing a rationale for your selection of literature, drawing points of comparison or conflict between texts, and providing critical commentary on the selected literature. The aim of the literature review is to persuade the reader that your research is informed, coherent, necessary and innovative. The literature review does not simply:

i) show that nothing has been written on the topic;

ii) show your awareness of the big names in the field;

iii) provide a summary of all the literature on the topic;

iv) introduce the reader to a pre-given field of research;

v) occur at the beginning of the research process;

vi) occur once all relevant material has been searched and copied

Original research does not mean being the first to examine a topic, but making a meaningful and useful contribution within a research community. If nothing has been written on the topic, it is your job to locate your research within a body of relevant literature. If you cannot find a relevant body of literature, it may be because the topic is not worth investigating.

6.7. Process of Writing Review of Literature

There are several steps to developing a literature review, but they are not necessarily sequential. You will probably find yourself moving backwards and forwards between them. The stages are:

i) Identify

ii) Record

iii) Ensure Relevance

iv) Retrieve

v) Review

vi) Write

6.7.1. Identify

Start by compiling a list of references and file the system that we will use - hard copy, an index system, a software referencing system, or a combination. Keeping your topic and questions in mind, you need to speak with your supervisor and other staff and students working in a similar area and ask them what they consider to be key readings relating to your topic.

Make an appointment with the liaison librarian and speak with them about the best retrieval systems and databases relating to our topic. Ask if there are any courses that we can attend on improving your effectiveness at online retrieval. You can also use the library's search strategies on-line tutorial to focus on the appropriate keywords and data sources. There are also a number of virtual libraries that may be useful. Work through the key catalogues, databases, indexes, bibliographies and websites for relevant resources. Check the references used in the articles you read, locate and use research reviews.

6.7.2. Record

Make a record of any literature that relates to your topic. At the very least you should have the citation details and where it is located (catalogue number, database, book shop). It is also a good idea to write a couple of sentences that will help you remember what the article is about. A tool that has been found to be useful is the reading log. Feel free to photocopy these so that there is one for every citation and then systematically file them in a folder.

6.7.3. Ensure Relevance

From reading the titles and abstracts, prioritise the literature that you have identified and make a note of why it has a high, medium or low priority. Develop the habit of screening the literature for relevance before we download it, print it out or order a hard copy. This way we will not become overwhelmed with all of the reading that we have to do.

Differentiate between textbooks, research articles and books, and books written for a non-academic audience. They contain different kinds of information that will be more or less relevant to our research proposal, or will be relevant in particular ways.

6.7.4. Retrieve

Make hard copies of the most important literature and work through this first. Print off relevant journal articles from the databases, photocopy articles (making sure you comply with copyright regulations) and borrow books. At this stage try to limit the number of books you buy - especially if you are on a budget.

Most of the literature we require will be available through the University. In addition to the online resources and direct lending facilities, we can also access inter-library loans and apply for reciprocal borrowing rights.

6.7.5. Review

It is useful to develop a systematic method for reviewing the literature. We can make up your own or use the reading log which allows us to record different kinds of information: the bibliographic details, a description, the relationship to other readings, our critical analysis, and any questions that it raises in terms of your own research. We can also record where the literature is located in our filing system or where we can access it. When taking notes be sure to be clear about when we are quoting and when we are paraphrasing. We cannot risk unintentionally plagiarizing ideas and information, the penalties are harsh and the damage to our reputation could be irreparable. Always keep the page numbers with anything taken from the literature so that we can easily check back to the quote or idea paraphrased when editing.

6.7.6. Write

The literature review has its own internal structure. It starts with an introductory paragraph; discusses the literature in a logical and coherent way; and concludes with a paragraph that relates the literature to the research project.

6.8. Constructing the Literature

The literature review actively constructs the field of your research. There are major ways that researchers construct their research fields. These are:

— *Synthesised Coherence*: It brings previously unrelated work together highlighting points of agreement in order to demonstrate the need for further investigation. In this mode the review highlights common concepts, methodologies, perspectives within apparently disparate fields of research.

— *Progressive Coherence*: It depicts the literature in terms of cumulative knowledge growth, consensus of perspectives and methods, and a well developed and focused line of inquiry. The current research is constructed as the next logical step in this collective and growing understanding of the topic.

— *Noncoherence*: It constructs the literature in terms of points of disagreement within a research program whose importance is commonly accepted. This approach emphasises both the continuous nature of the field, but also competing explanations, disputes, debates, or contradictions in the methodological approaches, findings of concepts adopted. The research situates itself within a contested field, and states its aims in terms of resolving or shedding light upon the debate.

6.8.1. Problematising Literature

Golden-Biddle and Lock summarise the key ways that researchers problematise the literature. These are as follows.

6.8.1.1. Incomplete

Here the literature is portrayed as not fully finished in some specific area. The research seeks to augment the field or fill a gap, rather than question its reigning paradigms in any significant way.

6.8.1.2. Inadequate

Here the literature is portrayed as excluding alternative perspectives. The research aims to contribute by bringing this oversight into view and introducing different views and frameworks. Existing paradigms are not so much questioned as extended and improved.

6.8.1.3. Incommensurate

Here existing research is portrayed as not simply incomplete, but wrong, or misguided in some way. The existing research seeks to overthrow existing views or paradigms in the field and to posit an alternative.

6.9. Shaping the Literature Review

You can avoid an approach that is purely descriptive, or one that simply passes judgment on the literature, by reading for major under currents and themes within the literature.

When reading relevant texts and writing the literature review you should ask some questions yourself. When you have solid answers to those questions you can be confident that your literature review and your research proposal are on firm ground.

6.10. Conclusion

Writing literature review is an active, critical and constructive exercise that forms an important part of mobilising your central thesis. You are not so much fitting yourself into an existing picture as painting a new picture. That is, the task is not simply one of locating yourself within an existing research community. Rather, the task is one of organising, reframing, and reconceptualising existing approaches in order to establish the importance of your own research.

REFERENCE

Golden-Biddle, K and Locke, K., *Composing Qualitative Research*, Sage: Thousand Oaks, 1997.

Rowley, J. and Slack, F., "Conducting a Literature Review", *Management Research News*, 2004.

7

Designing Research

7.1. Introduction

A design is used to structure the research, to show how all of the major parts of the research project—the samples or groups, measures, treatments or programmes, and methods of assignment—work together to try to address the central research questions. Research design can be thought of as the structure of research—it is the "glue" that holds all of the elements in a research project together. A design using is a concise notation that enables us to summarise a complex design structure efficiently.

7.2. Elements of Research Design

The following are the elements of a design:

7.2.1. Observations or Measures

These are symbolised by an 'O' in design notation. An O can refer to a single measure (e.g., a measure of body weight), a single instrument with multiple items (e.g., a 10-item self-esteem scale), a complex multi-part instrument (e.g., a survey), or a whole battery of tests or measures given out on one occasion. If you need to distinguish among specific measures, you can use subscripts with the O, as in O_1, O_2, and so on.

7.2.2. Treatments or Programmes

These are symbolised with an 'X' in design notations. The X can refer to a simple intervention (e.g., a one-time surgical technique) or to a complex hodgepodge programme (e.g., an employment training programme). Usually, a no-treatment control or comparison group has no symbol for the treatment (some researchers use X+ and X- to indicate the treatment and control respectively). As with observations, you can use subscripts to distinguish different programmes or programme variations.

7.2.3. Groups

Each group in a design is given its own line in the design structure. If the design notation has three lines, there are three groups in the design.

7.2.3.1. Assignment to Group

Assignment to group is designated by a letter at the beginning of each line (i.e., group) that describes how the group was assigned. The major types of assignment are:

— R = random assignment
— N = nonequivalent groups
— C = assignment by cutoff

7.2.4. Time

Time moves from left to right. Elements that are listed on the left occur before elements that are listed on the right.

7.3. Design Notation

There are two lines in the notation, so you should realise that the study has two groups. There are four Os in the notation, two on each line and two for each group. When the Os are stacked vertically on top of each other it means they are collected at the same time. In the notation we have two Os that are taken before (i.e., to the left of) any treatment is given—the pretest—and two Os taken after the treatment is given—the post-test.

The R at the beginning of each line signifies that the two groups are randomly assigned (making it an experimental design). The design is a treatment versus comparison group one because the top line (treatment group) has an X while the bottom line (control group) does not. Sometimes we have to be more specific in describing the Os or Xs than just using a single letter. With this simple set of rules for describing a research design in notational form, you can concisely explain even complex design structures. And, using a notation helps to show common design sub-structures across different designs that we might not recognise as easily without the notation.

7.4. Types of Designs

We can classify designs into a simple threefold classification by asking some key questions.

First, does the design use random assignment to groups? If random assignment is used, we call the design a randomised experiment or true experiment. If random assignment is not used, then we have to ask a second question: Does the design use either multiple groups or multiple waves of measurement? If the answer is yes, we would label it a quasi-experimental design. If no, we would call it a non-experimental design. This threefold classification is especially useful for describing the design with respect to internal validity. A randomised experiment generally is the strongest of the three designs when your interest is in establishing a cause-effect relationship.

The second design is a pre-post nonequivalent groups quasi-experiment. We know it's not a randomised experiment because random assignment wasn't used. And we know it's not a non-experiment because there are both multiple groups and multiple waves of measurement. That means it must be a quasi-experiment.

A non-experiment is generally the weakest in this respect. In fact, the simplest form of non-experiment is a one-shot survey design that consists of nothing but a single observation O. This is probably one of the most common forms of research and, for some research questions—especially descriptive ones—is clearly a strong design.

7.4.1. Experimental Design

Experimental designs are often touted as the most "rigorous" of all research designs or, as the "gold standard" against which all other designs are judged. In one sense, they probably are. If you can implement an experimental design well (and that is a big "if" indeed), then the experiment is probably the strongest design with respect to internal validity. Recall that internal validity is at the center of all causal or cause-effect inferences. When you want to determine whether some programme or treatment causes some outcome or outcomes to occur, then you are interested in having strong internal validity.

In the simplest type of experiment, we create two groups that are "equivalent" to each other. One group (the programme or treatment group) gets the programme and the other group (the comparison or control group) does not. In all other respects, the groups are treated the same. They have similar people, live in similar contexts, have similar backgrounds, and so on. Now, if we observe differences in outcomes between these two groups, then the differences must be due to the only thing that differs between them—that one got the programme and the other didn't.

The approach used in experimental design is to assign people randomly from a common pool of people into the two groups. The experiment relies on this idea of random assignment to groups as the basis for obtaining two groups that are similar.

The key to the success of the experiment is in the random assignment. In fact, even with random assignment we never expect that the groups we create will be exactly the same. So, if we randomly assign people to two groups, and we have enough people in our study to achieve the desired probabilistic equivalence, then we may consider the experiment to be strong in internal validity and we probably have a good shot at assessing whether the programme causes the outcome(s).

The experimental design is intrusive and difficult to carry out in most real world contexts. And, because an experiment is often an intrusion, you are to some extent setting up an artificial situation so that you can assess your causal relationship with high internal validity. If so, then you are limiting the degree to which you can generalise your results to real contexts where you haven't set up an experiment. That is, you have reduced your external validity in order to achieve greater internal validity.

If the situation is right, an experiment can be a very strong design to use. But it isn't automatically so. Experimental design is a fairly complex subject in its own right. But there are lots of experimental design variations that attempt to accomplish different things or solve different problems.

7.4.2. Quasi-Experimental Design

A quasi-experimental design is one that looks a bit like an experimental design but lacks the key ingredient—random assignment. With respect to internal validity, they often appear to be inferior to randomised experiments. But there is something compelling about these designs; taken as a group, they are easily more frequently implemented than their randomised cousins.

Probably the most commonly used quasi-experimental design (and it may be the most commonly used of all designs) is the nonequivalent groups design. In its simplest form it requires a pretest and post-test for a treated and comparison group.

7.4.3. Random Selection and Assignment

Random selection is how you draw the sample of people for your study from a population. Random assignment is how you assign the sample that you draw to different groups or treatments in your study.

It is possible to have both random selection and assignment in a study. Let's say you drew a random sample of 100 clients from a population list of 1000 current clients of your organisation. That is random sampling. Now, let's say you randomly assign 50 of these clients to get some new additional treatment and the other 50 to be controls. That's random assignment.

It is also possible to have only one of these (random selection or random assignment) but not the other in a study. For instance, if you do not randomly draw the 100 cases from your list of 1000 but instead just take the first 100 on the list, you do not have random selection. But you could still randomly assign this nonrandom sample to treatment versus control. Or, you could randomly select 100 from your list of 1000 and then nonrandomly (haphazardly) assign them to treatment or control.

And, it's possible to have neither random selection nor random assignment. In a typical nonequivalent groups design in education you might nonrandomly choose two 5th grade classes to be in your study. This is nonrandom selection. Then, you could arbitrarily assign one to get the new educational programme and the other to be the control. This is nonrandom (or nonequivalent) assignment.

Random selection is related to sampling. Therefore it is most related to the external validity (or generalisability) of your results. After all, we would randomly sample so that our research participants better represent the larger group from which they're drawn. Random assignment is most related to design. In fact, when we randomly assign participants to treatments we have, by definition, an experimental design. Therefore, random assignment is most related to internal validity. After all, we randomly assign in order to help assure that our treatment groups are similar to each other (i.e., equivalent) prior to the treatment.

7.4.4. Pre-Post Designs

There are three major types of pre-post programme-comparison group designs all sharing the basic design structure shown in the notation above:

— The Randomised Experimental (RE) Design
— The Nonequivalent Group (NEGD) Design
— The Regression-Discontinuity (RD) Design

The designs differ in the method by which participants are assigned to the two groups. In the RE, participants are assigned randomly. In the RD design, they are assigned using a cutoff score on the pretest. In the NEGD, assignment of participants is not explicitly controlled—they may self select into either group, or other unknown or unspecified factors may determine assignment.

Because these three designs differ so critically in their assignment strategy, they are often considered distinct or unrelated. But it is useful to look at them as forming a continuum, both in terms of assignment and in terms of their strength with respect to internal validity.

7.5. Designing Designs for Research

Much contemporary social research is devoted to examining whether a programme, treatment, or manipulation causes some outcome or result. For example, we might wish to know whether a new educational programme causes subsequent achievement score gains, whether a special work release programme for prisoners causes lower recidivism rates, whether a novel drug causes a reduction in symptoms, and so on. There are three conditions must be met before we can infer that such a cause-effect relation exists:

1. *Covariation*. Changes in the presumed cause must be related to changes in the presumed effect. Thus, if we introduce, remove, or change the level of a treatment or programme, we should observe some change in the outcome measures.
2. *Temporal Precedence*. The presumed cause must occur prior to the presumed effect.
3. *No Plausible Alternative Explanations*. The presumed cause must be the only reasonable explanation for changes in the outcome measures. If there are other factors which could be responsible for changes in the outcome measures we cannot be confident that the presumed cause-effect relationship is correct.

In most social research the third condition is the most difficult to meet. Any number of factors other than the treatment or programme could cause changes in outcome measures. Standard social science methodology textbooks typically present an array of research designs and the alternative explanations which these designs rule out or minimise. This tends to foster a "cookbook" approach to research design - an emphasis on the selection of an available design rather than on the construction of an appropriate research strategy. While standard designs may sometimes fit real-life situations, it will often be necessary to "tailor" a research design to minimise specific threats to validity. Furthermore, even if standard textbook designs are used, an understanding of the logic of design construction in general will improve the comprehension of these standard approaches.

7.5.1. Ways to Minimise Threats

Good research designs minimise the plausible alternative explanations for the hypothesised cause-effect relationship. But such explanations may be ruled out or minimised in a number of ways other than by design. The discussion which follows outlines five ways to minimise threats to validity, one of which is by research design:

1. *By Argument*. The most straightforward way to rule out a potential threat to validity is to simply argue that the threat in question is not a reasonable one. Such an argument may be made either a priori or a posteriori, although the former will usually be more convincing than the latter. For example, depending on the situation, one might argue that an instrumentation threat is not likely because the same test is used for pre and post test measurements and did not involve observers who might improve, or other such factors. In most cases, ruling out a potential threat to validity by argument alone will be weaker than the other approaches listed below. As a result, the most plausible threats in a study should not, except in unusual cases, be ruled out by argument only.
2. *By Measurement or Observation*. In some cases it will be possible to rule out a threat by measuring it and demonstrating that either it does not occur at all or occurs so minimally as to not be a strong alternative explanation for the cause-effect relationship. Consider, for example, a study of the effects of an advertising campaign on subsequent sales of a particular product. In such a study, history (i.e., the occurrence of other events which might lead to an increased desire to purchase the product) would be a plausible alternative explanation. For example, a change in the local economy, the removal of a competing product from the market, or similar events could cause an increase in product sales. One might attempt to minimise such threats by measuring local economic indicators and the availability and sales of competing products. If there is no change in these measures coincident with the onset of the advertising campaign, these threats would be considerably minimised. Similarly, if one is studying the effects of special mathematics training on math achievement scores of children, it might be useful to observe everyday classroom behaviour in order to verify that students were not receiving any additional math training to that provided in the study.
3. *By Design*. Here, the major emphasis is on ruling out alternative explanations by adding treatment or control

groups, waves of measurement, and the like. This topic will be discussed in more detail below.

4. *By Analysis*. There are a number of ways to rule out alternative explanations using statistical analysis. One interesting example is provided by Jurs and Glass. They suggest that one could study the plausibility of an attrition or mortality threat by conducting a two-way analysis of variance. One factor in this study would be the original treatment group designations (i.e., programme vs. comparison group), while the other factor would be attrition (i.e., dropout vs. non-dropout group). The dependent measure could be the pretest or other available pre-programme measures. A main effect on the attrition factor would be indicative of a threat to external validity or generalisability, while an interaction between group and attrition factors would point to a possible threat to internal validity. Where both effects occur, it is reasonable to infer that there is a threat to both internal and external validity.

   The plausibility of alternative explanations might also be minimised using covariance analysis. For example, in a study of the effects of "workfare" programmes on social welfare case loads, one plausible alternative explanation might be the status of local economic conditions. Here, it might be possible to construct a measure of economic conditions and include that measure as a covariate in the statistical analysis. One must be careful when using covariance adjustments of this type—"perfect" covariates do not exist in most social research and the use of imperfect covariates will not completely adjust for potential alternative explanations. Nevertheless causal assertions are likely to be strengthened by demonstrating that treatment effects occur even after adjusting on a number of good covariates.

5. *By Preventive Action*. When potential threats are anticipated they can often be ruled out by some type of preventive action. For example, if the programme is a desirable one, it is likely that the comparison group would feel jealous or demoralised. Several actions can be taken to minimise the effects of these attitudes including offering the programme

to the comparison group upon completion of the study or using programme and comparison groups which have little opportunity for contact and communication. In addition, auditing methods and quality control can be used to track potential experimental dropouts or to insure the standardisation of measurement.

The five categories listed above should not be considered mutually exclusive. The inclusion of measurements designed to minimise threats to validity will obviously be related to the design structure and is likely to be a factor in the analysis. In general, reducing a particular threat by design or preventive action will probably be stronger than by using one of the other three approaches. The choice of which strategy to use for any particular threat is complex and depends at least on the cost of the strategy and on the potential seriousness of the threat.

7.6. Elements of Design Construction

Most research designs can be constructed from four basic elements:

1. *Time.* A causal relationship, by its very nature, implies that some time has elapsed between the occurrence of the cause and the consequent effect. While for some phenomena the elapsed time might be measured in microseconds and therefore might be unnoticeable to a casual observer, we normally assume that the cause and effect in social science arenas do not occur simultaneously, In design notation we indicate this temporal element horizontally - whatever symbol is used to indicate the presumed cause would be placed to the left of the symbol indicating measurement of the effect. Thus, as we read from left to right in design notation we are reading across time. Complex designs might involve a lengthy sequence of observations and programmes or treatments across time.
2. *Programme(s) or Treatment(s).* The presumed cause may be a programme or treatment under the explicit control of the researcher or the occurrence of some natural event or programme not explicitly controlled. In design notation we usually depict a presumed cause with the symbol "X". When multiple programmes or treatments are being

studied using the same design, we can keep the programmes distinct by using subscripts such as "X1" or "X2". For a comparison group (i.e., one which does not receive the programme under study) no "X" is used.

3. *Observation(s) or Measure(s).* Measurements are typically depicted in design notation with the symbol "O". If the same measurement or observation is taken at every point in time in a design, then this "O" will be sufficient. Similarly, if the same set of measures is given at every point in time in this study, the "O" can be used to depict the entire set of measures. However, if different measures are given at different times it is useful to subscript the "O" to indicate which measurement is being given at which point in time.
4. *Groups or Individuals.* The final design element consists of the intact groups or the individuals who participate in various conditions. Typically, there will be one or more programme and comparison groups. In design notation, each group is indicated on a separate line. Furthermore, the manner in which groups are assigned to the conditions can be indicated by an appropriate symbol at the beginning of each line. Here, "R" will represent a group which was randomly assigned, "N" will depict a group which was nonrandomly assigned (i.e., a nonequivalent group or cohort) and a "C" will indicate that the group was assigned using a cutoff score on a measurement.

7.6.1. A Strategy for Design Construction

Considering the basic elements of a research design or the possibilities for expansion are not alone sufficient. We need to be able to integrate these elements with an overall strategy. Furthermore we need to decide which potential threats are best handled by design rather than by argument, measurement, analysis, or preventive action.

While no definitive approach for designing designs exists, we might suggest a tentative strategy based on the notion of expansion discussed above. First, we begin the designing task by setting forth a design which depicts the simple hypothesised causal relationship. Second, we deliberately over-expand this basic design by expanding across time, programme, observations, and groups. At this step, the emphasis is on accounting for as many likely alternative explanations as possible using the design. Finally, we then scale back this over-expanded version considering the effect of eliminating each design component. It is at this point that we face the difficult decisions concerning the costs of each design component and the advantages of ruling out specific threats using other approaches.

There are several advantages which result from using this type of approach to design construction. First, we are forced to be explicit about the decisions which are made. Second, the approach is "conservative" in nature. The strategy minimises the chance of our overlooking a major threat to validity in constructing our design. Third, we arrive at a design which is "tailored" to the situation at hand. Finally, the strategy is cost-efficient. Threats which can be accounted for by some other, less costly, approach need not be accounted for in the design itself.

7.7. Characteristics of Good Research Design

Throughout the design construction task, it is important to have in mind some endpoint, some criteria which we should try to achieve before finally accepting a design strategy. The criteria discussed below are only meant to be suggestive of the characteristics found in good research design. It is worth noting that all of these criteria point to the need to individually tailor research designs rather than accepting standard textbook strategies as is.

1. *Theory-Grounded*. Good research strategies reflect the theories which are being investigated. Where specific theoretical expectations can be hypothesised these are incorporated into the design. For example, where theory predicts a specific treatment effect on one measure but not on another, the inclusion of both in the design improves discriminant validity and demonstrates the predictive power of the theory.
2. *Situational*. Good research designs reflect the settings of the investigation. This was illustrated above where a particular need of teachers and administrators was explicitly addressed in the design strategy. Similarly, intergroup

rivalry, demoralisation, and competition might be assessed through the use of additional comparison groups who are not in direct contact with the original group.

3. *Feasible*. Good designs can be implemented. The sequence and timing of events are carefully thought out. Potential problems in measurement, adherence to assignment, database construction and the like, are anticipated. Where needed, additional groups or measurements are included in the design to explicitly correct for such problems.
4. *Redundant*. Good research designs have some flexibility built into them. Often, this flexibility results from duplication of essential design features. For example, multiple replications of a treatment help to insure that failure to implement the treatment in one setting will not invalidate the entire study.
5. *Efficient*. Good designs strike a balance between redundancy and the tendency to overdesign. Where it is reasonable, other, less costly, strategies for ruling out potential threats to validity are utilised.

This is by no means an exhaustive list of the criteria by which we can judge good research design. nevertheless, goals of this sort help to guide the researcher toward a final design choice and emphasise important components which should be included.

The development of a theory of research methodology for the social sciences has largely occurred over the past half century and most intensively within the past two decades. It is not surprising, in such a relatively recent effort, that an emphasis on a few standard research designs has occurred. Nevertheless, by moving away from the notion of "design selection" and towards an emphasis on design construction, there is much to be gained in our understanding of design principles and in the quality of our research.

7.8. Conclusion

Design research investigates the process of designing in all its many fields. It is thus related to Design methods in general or for particular disciplines. A primary interpretation of design research is that it is concerned with undertaking research into the design process. Secondary interpretations would refer to undertaking research *within* the process of design. The overall intention is to better understand and to improve the design process.

References

Boruch, R.F., "Coupling randomized experiments and approximations to experiments in social program evaluation", *Sociological Methods and Research*, 1975.

Campbell, D.T. and Stanley, J.C., *Experimental and Quasi-Experimental Designs for Research*, Rand McNally, Chicago, Illinois, 1963, 1966.

Cook, T.D. and Campbell, D.T., *Quasi-Experimentation: Design and Analysis for Field Settings*, Rand McNally, Chicago, Illinois, 1979.

Cross, N (ed.), *Developments in Design Methodology*, Chichester, UK: John Wiley & Sons Ltd., 1984.

Judd, C.M. and Kenny, D.A., *Estimating the Effects of Social Interventions*, Cambridge University Press, Cambridge, MA., 1981.

Laurel, B., *Design Research: Methods and Perspectives*, Cambridge: M.I.T. Press, 2003.

8

Methods of Educational Research

Research is a systematic, formal rigorous and precise process employed to gain solutions to problems and/or to discover and interpret new facts and relationships. It is the process of looking for a specific answer to a specific question in an organised objective reliable way.

Research is the instrument used to test whether a theory is good or not. It is the method by which data is gathered to generate a theory or to test a theory. There are different ways of conducting research, however any method you use will be based on the systematic collection and analysis of data. Research is finding out what you don't already know. No one knows everything, but everybody knows something. However, to complicate matters, often what you know, or think you know, is incorrect.

There are two basic purposes for research: to learn something, or to gather evidence. The first, to learn something, is for your own benefit. It is almost impossible for a human to stop learning. Research is organised learning, looking for specific things to add to your store of knowledge.

8.1. Types of Research

There are three types of research, pure, original, and secondary. Each type has the goal of finding information and/or understanding something. The difference comes in the strategy employed in achieving the objective.

8.1.1. Pure Research

Pure research is research done simply to find out something by examining anything. For instance, in some pure scientific research scientists discover what properties various materials possess. It is not for the sake of applying those properties to anything in particular, but simply to find out what properties there are. Pure mathematics is for the sake of seeing what happens, not to solve a problem. The fun of pure research is that you are not looking for anything in particular. Instead, anything and everything you find may be joined with anything else just to see where that combination would lead, if anywhere.

8.1.2. Original Research

Original or primary research is looking for information that nobody else has found. Observing people's response to advertising, how prison sentences influence crime rates, doing tests, observations, experiments, etc., are to discover something new. Original research requires two things:

i) Knowing what has already been discovered, having a background on the subject; and

ii) Formulating a method to find out what you want to know. To accomplish the first you indulge in secondary research.

For the second, you decide how best to find the information you need to arrive at a conclusion. This method may be using focus groups, interviews, observations, expeditions, experiments, surveys, etc.

8.1.3. Secondary Research

Secondary research is finding out what others have discovered through original research and trying to reconcile conflicting viewpoints or conclusions, find new relationships between normally non-related research, and arrive at your own conclusion based on others' work. This is, of course, the usual course for college students.

Secondary research should not be belittled simply because it is not original research. Fresh insights and viewpoints, based on a wide variety of facts gleaned from original research in many areas, has often been a source of new ideas. Even more, it has provided a clearer understanding of what the evidence means without the influence of the original researcher's prejudices and preconceptions.

Research, pure, original or secondary, carries with it an inherent danger to those who are close-minded or comfortable in their preconceptions and prejudices. In case you're wondering, that includes everybody. However, there are people who, having arrived at a conclusion by whatever means, reject anything that contradicts, or at least doesn't support, their preconceptions and prejudices. Research has at its essence the shakeup of what you already know. Let's take a look at how this works.

Research may show that what you already know isn't correct. This is a hard thing for many people to accept. You will, on occasion, come across a piece of evidence that contradicts your a priori assumptions (those that you hold as self-evident, some thing is simply because it is), and that is at best disconcerting and at worst traumatic.

8.1.4. Directed and Non-directed Research

Research can be directed or non-directed. Non-directed research is finding out things for the sheer fun of finding them out. Watching television is non-directed research, as is reading a magazine, science fiction, mysteries, historical fiction, or anything else. Everything you don't think of yourself contains information you don't have, and is thus research.

Directed research, on the other hand, is done with a specific purpose in mind. The purpose could be to make a point, write a paper or speech, or simply know more about a specific thing. It is directed since it deals with something specific, and someone decides what to try next. It simply doesn't have a specific outcome in mind. For example, directed research in microelectronics is not trying to achieve a specific goal. It does, however, deal specifically with microelectronics, be it the conducting properties of alloys and compounds, electron etching, or dual bonding. It does not concern itself with anthropology. There is also a researcher or project director who decides what is worth pursuing and what is not.

Directed research is what you want to do when you are preparing a report. You have a specific goal in mind, to communicate what you want your audience to know about your topic. Thus, you direct your research toward finding what you can about your topic, not to find out what there is to know about whatever you come across.

8.2. Process of Research

To know from where to find evidence and how to find it is the most difficult step for most people. They spend days and even weeks finding information to use in their papers or speeches. With a little thought and planning it is possible to cut that time down to hours. This is true whether you are an undergraduate having to do an English paper or public speaking assignment, a graduate student needing a review of literature, or a professional needing to do a report or speech for work.

8.2.1 Choose a Topic

The first step is determining your specific topic. There are many subjects, but each subject has many topics. For example, the subject may be geology, but your topic may be granite, igneous formations, or volcanism. You can narrow down each of these topics even more specifically. You can narrow volcanism to cone formation, ash versus lava volcanoes, dome formation, relationship of earthquakes to volcanism, etc.

8.2.2. Brainstorming

The process of selecting a topic is called brainstorming. Brainstorming makes it sound like you're doing something extremely powerful with your mind. You are doing something extremely powerful with your mind: you are allowing your mind to do what it is most capable of doing-synthesising. It is allowing the mind to work at random, to find relationships between ideas and concepts by utilising the subconscious rather than the conscious mind.

Brainstorming can start anywhere. Simply look around the room, pick an object, say it or write it down, write down the next word that occurs to you without trying to think of one, then write down the next word that occurs to you, then the next, then the next, then the next. Do this until nothing occurs to you, or until your hand falls off from writer's cramp, which ever comes first.

Another great advantage to this ideation or brainstorming is the fact that if you did not already know something about the topic it would never occur to you to write it down; it simply would not come into your mind. Thus, you can avoid a great deal of time and effort spent learning enough about a topic to decide whether or not you want to do it or not: you already know enough about the topic to be able to start your outline.

This latter point, that prior knowledge about a topic must be in your mind for the topic to occur to you, is the greatest reason and the greatest power of brainstorming. When you start to outline you will find that you already know enough about the topic to be able to do at least two levels of your outline. This is a great saving in time, effort, and research.

The next step in brainstorming is simply elimination. You want to remove from your list of topics anything that 1) you're not interested in; 2) is too much trouble; 3) you feel you don't know enough about; 4) your audience wouldn't be interested in; or 5) you just don't care. Don't take this last too lightly: if you don't care about your topic, neither will your audience.

The easiest way to eliminate possible topics is to go to the top of your list and brainstorm about each individual topic. Do it quickly: if nothing occurs to you when you look at it, strike it out. If something does occur to you to narrow down your topic or specify it, apply to it the same rules as above. If it's too complicated for your audience, does not fulfill the assignment, or you just aren't interested in discussing that topic, then strike it out.

8.2.3 Beginning the Research

The second step also uses brainstorming. Make a list of every major thing you know about your topic. Then for each item on the list put whatever support you can brainstorm for them. In this way you find out how much you already know about your topic. You may discover one of three things. First, you already know a lot more than you thought and thus will have an easy time finding evidence. Second, you don't know as much as you thought and therefore will have to learn more before trying to report it. Third, what you know is contradictory and you will have to do research to understand your topic. In any case, you're not wasting time in libraries or labs finding out what you already know.

Once you've reached this point it is time to plan your research. Examine your list for holes. Are there some main ideas that have only one or no pieces of support? You'll either have to eliminate or research that main idea. Are there some sub points that have little or no evidence? You'll have to find some: a sub point cannot stand alone. Is a sub point or piece of evidence your opinion only? You must find some other evidence to back it up.

8.3. Preparing a Research Plan

There are twelve steps to prepare a research report or a thesis.

8.3.1. Reporting the Problem

It all starts with an idea we might have as to what kind of a problem we want to solve or what question we might want to answer. As professionals in education or in related fields our everyday practices constantly bring up questions we might want to answer. We can also come up with excellent topics for a research project by reading widely in the professional journals in our field and also by pursuing introductory textbooks in our area of specialisation.

8.3.2. Define all Variables

Once we have identified a research problem we will want to clearly state operational definitions for all variables. In some cases we might have to provide tentative operational definitions until we have done an extensive review of the related literature.

8.3.3. Formation of Keywords

Before you begin your search for articles and other materials relevant to research topic, you have to generate the keywords you will use for your search. These keywords can include, in addition to the content of your research topic, words representing the variables in your research and the categorical representation of the subjects you intend to use in your research (e.g. gifted students with learning disabilities—could use keywords gifted learning disabled).

8.3.4. Search for Relevant Literature

With your keywords in hand you can begin to search a database for articles and other materials relevant to your research topic. You will also want to use other resources such as the Encyclopedia of Educational Research and the Review of Educational Research.

8.3.5. Prepare Brief of Each Relevant Article

As you read the relevant literature you will want to take notes and paraphrase what you have read, to include in your literature review. You can also mark your notes with some sort of a code so that you can retrieve the note by its code.

8.3.6. Outline Article Codes

Before you write your review of the literature it is a good idea to create an outline for your review and then enter your article codes in to the outline. This should put you in good shape to actually write your review.

8.3.7. Prepare Review of Related Literature

While you write review of the related literature, use your notes and outline to assist you, you should end up suggesting, implying, or in some way pointing toward your research hypothesis.

8.3.8. Formulate Research Hypothesis

Your research hypothesis should clearly state the relationship that you conclude exists between the variables, particularly the independent and dependent variables. You should also include a definition of each variable in operational, measurable terms.

8.3.9. Make Research Plan or Proposal

The next step is to actually prepare the formal research plan or proposal. The target goal for this course is to prepare a formal research plan or proposal. You will eventually want to actually do the study you have proposed, so you must go on to the next step of the process.

8.3.10. Get Permissions to Conduct Study

You will need to get permission to conduct your study in the public or private schools. Your advisor can be of assistance to you in this, but either or both of you must contact the chief school administrator for permission to conduct research in the school. With the top level blessing you will then be able to proceed to the building level and secure the permission of the building principal and of the teachers or other staff members who will be involved in or impacted by your research. Finally you will need to secure the permission of the subjects of your study themselves (if eighteen or older) or of the parents or legal guardians of students under the age of 18. This is a legal requirement imposed on anyone who does research.

8.3.11. Start the Study

With all of the above done, you are finally ready to conduct your research.

8.3.12. Prepare the Final Report

With your research conducted, you are ready to prepare the final report or thesis, that your research generated.

8.4. Structure of Research Plan

Your research proposal or plan will have the following format. Some of these items you have already completed. You must need to fulfill the specifications before submitting the final proposal for your research plan.

8.4.1. Selection of the Subject

The way in which we select subjects for a study determines how we are able to generalise the results of our study.

8.4.1.1. Population and Sample

Population is an entire group of persons or elements that have at least one thing in common. Sample is a small group of persons or elements (observations) selected from the total population. We want the sample to be representative of the population, so we need to use a sampling method that will achieve this. Sampling methods is the methods of selecting a sample from the population.

— *Simple random sampling:* equal chance for each member of the group to be selected

— *Systematic sampling:* selecting every 10th member (for example) from an alphabetised list

— *Stratified sample:* dividing the population into subgroups and then randomly selecting from among these subgroups.

Number selected from each subgroup can be proportional or equal-sized.

— *Cluster sampling:* groups are selected rather than individuals.

— *Incidental or convenience sampling:* with this type of sampling, just take any group that you have access to. This, of course, will cause problems in generalising the results of your study.

8.4.1.2 *Determination of Sample Size*

— Samples should be as large as possible; in general, the larger the sample, the more representative it is likely to be, and the more generalisable the results of the study are likely to be.

— Minimum, acceptable sizes depend on the type of research. Generally you would need 30 subjects in each group for correlational and descriptive research but may be able to get by with 15 subjects per group in experimental or quasi-experimental designs.

— Even large samples can lead to erroneous conclusions if they are not well selected.

— The authors of your text provide a table based on work of Krejcie and Morgan which shows recommended sample sizes based on various population sizes.

8.4.1.3. *Bias in Sampling*

Sampling bias is caused by systematic errors (rather than random errors), in the sampling process.

8.4.2. Collection and Coding Data

Data collection must be accurate, where tests are used they must be scored correctly, and observations must be made systematically. In some cases data may be coded—for example males coded as 1 and females coded as 2.

An electronic spreadsheet is an excellent place to keep the data for your study, both raw data and coded data. In most cases you will also be able to perform the desired statistical calculations from within the spreadsheet. There are three major ways to collect data.

i) Administer a standardised instrument

ii) Administer a self-developed instrument

iii) Record naturally available data

8.4.3. Selecting a Standardised Test

Standardised tests of one sort or another are used in most educational research studies. You will frequently use standardised tests to measure one or more of the variables in your study. It is important that you get as much information as you can about the tests that you are going to use in your study. In some cases no suitable instrument exists to measure the variables of your study. In that case you will have to design your own instrument. Many of the parameters on which standardised tests are rated, will not be available for an instrument you design.

8.4.3.1. Characteristics of Standardised Tests

i) *Validity:* The validity of a test is a measure of how well a test measures what it is supposed to measure. The examiner's manual or technical manual for most tests will have information on the validity of the test.

ii) *Reliability:* Reliability is a measure of how consistent the results from a test are.

There are many different types of tests that you might consider using in your study. Some of the most commonly used types of tests for educational research are:

a) Achievement tests

b) Personality tests

c) Aptitude tests, including tests of academic aptitude (intelligence tests)

There are many sources available, in most university libraries to assist you in identifying an appropriate test to use in your study and also to provide evaiuative information about a test you would like to use. You should avail yourself of one or more of these sources to assist you as you design your research study.

iii) *Mental Measurement Yearbooks:* These periodically updated year books contain extensive information about most kinds of tests. In addition to technical information about the tests, they include critical reviews of the tests.

iv) *Tests in Print:* Tests is Print is frequently updated and is a good source to initiallly look at for information on a test. It provides references to the appropriate Mental Measurement Yearbook for more information on the test.

v) *Test Critiques:* Test Critiques are another source of information about tests you may wish to look at.

8.4.4. Types of Research Designs

Once you have formulated a research problem, conducted a review of related research, formulated a research hypothesis, described a sample (subjects), and selected one or more measuring instruments you are ready to prepare the methods section of your research proposal or report. The methods section of your proposal should include sections on

— A description of the subjects

— A description of the instruments to be used in the study

— A description of the research design

— A description of the specific procedures to be followed in your study

The methods section of your study will be followed by a description of methods you intend to use to analyse your data.

8.5. Historical Research

Historical Research is the systematic collection and objective evaluation of data related to past occurrences in order to test hypotheses concerning causes, effects, or trends of these events that may help to explain present events and anticipate future events.

8.5.1. Steps for Conducting Historical Research

The process for conducting historical research is the same as for other research.

— Definition of a problem
— Formulation of questions to be answered or hypotheses to be tested
— Systematic collection of data
— Evaluation of data
— Production of a verbal synthesis of findings or confirmation/disconfirmation of hypotheses.

8.6. Qualitative Research

Qualitative Research involves intensive data collection (lots of many variables), over an extended period of time, in a naturalistic setting (variables are studied when and where they naturally occur). Sometimes qualitative research is called naturalistic inquiry or field studies.

This type of research goes by many names: ethnography, cognitive anthropology, etc. A good way to understand qualitative research is to examine it in terms of the research parameters we've already discussed:

8.6.1. General Approach

First, qualitative research tends to be synthetic rather than analytic. It attempts to capture "the big picture" and see how a multitude of variables work together in the real world.

8.6.2. Research Aim

Another characteristic of qualitative research is that it is generally heuristic or hypothesis generating. Unlike deductive research, it does not start with preconceived notions or hypotheses, attempting to discover, understand, and interpret what is happening in the research context.

8.6.3. Handling of Research Context

In addition, the degree of control over the research context is low. Qualitative research examines naturally occurring behaviour, so the investigative methods are as non-intrusive as possible.

Therefore, the researcher's effect on the subjects and the data is minimal.

8.6.4. Openness of Data Collection Procedures

The level of explicitness in data collection procedures is also low. The data are more impressionistic and interpretive than numerical.

8.7. Descriptive Research

Descriptive research, also known as statistical research, describes data and characteristics about the population or phenomenon being studied. Descriptive research answers the questions who, what, where, when and how. Although the data description is factual, accurate and systematic, the research cannot describe what caused a situation. Thus, descriptive research cannot be used to create a causal relationship, where one variable affects another. In other words, descriptive research can be said to have a low requirement for internal validity.

The description is used for frequencies, averages and other statistical calculations. Often the best approach, prior to writing descriptive research, is to conduct a survey investigation. Qualitative research often has the aim of description and researchers may follow-up with examinations of why the observations exist and what the implications of the findings are.

This type of research is also a grouping that includes many particular research methodologies and procedures, such as observations, surveys, self-reports, and tests. The four parameters of research will help us understand how descriptive research in general is similar to, and different from, other types of research.

8.7.1. General Approach

Unlike qualitative research, descriptive research may be more analytic. It often focuses on a particular variable or factor.

8.7.2 Objective of the Research

Descriptive research may also operate on the basis of hypotheses (often generated through previous, qualitative research). That moves it toward the deductive side of the deductive/heuristic continuum.

8.7.3. Managing Research Context

Finally, like qualitative research, descriptive research aims to gather data without any manipulation of the research context. In other words, descriptive research is also low on the "control or manipulation of research context" scale. It is non-intrusive and deals with naturally occurring phenomena.

8.7.4. Nature of Data Collection Procedures

In addition, the data collection procedures used in descriptive research may be very explicit. Some observation instruments, for example, employ highly refined categories of behaviour and yield quantitative (numerical) data. These differences also lead to another significant characteristic of descriptive research-the types of subjects it studies.

Descriptive research may focus on individual subjects and go into great depth and detail in describing them. Individual variation is not only allowed for but studied. This approach is called a case-study. On the other hand, because of the data collection and analysis procedures (such as surveys) it may employ, descriptive research can also investigate large groups of subjects. Often these are pre-existing classes. In these cases, the analytical procedures tend to produce results that show "average" behaviour for the group.

8.7.5. Undertaking a Descriptive Research

The process of conducting a descriptive research study would include the following:

i) State the hypotheses or questions you hope to answer with your descriptive study.
ii) Define subjects.
iii) Develop the instrumentation for your study. Usually this involves selecting or more often developing a questionnaire.
iv) Validate the questionnaire.
v) Prepare a cover letter
vi) Pretest the questionnaire

vii) Plan how you will deal with non-respondents and with items not completed

viii) Description and analysis of results

8.7.6. Types of Self-report Research

Some of the common types of self-report research are:

i) Survey Research -a survey is an attempt to collect data from members of a population in order to determine the current status of that population with respect to one or more variables.

   a) Sample survey—simple random sample or stratified random sample.

   b) Census survey—entire population is surveyed

ii) Developmental studies

   — Cross sectional approach—different ages of subjects are studied at the same time.

   — Longitudinal approach—follow up a single group of subjects.

iii) Follow-up studies

iv) Sociometric studies

8.8. Correlational Research

The basic question for descriptive research is—"What are the values of a number of variables for a given sample of subjects. The basic research question for correlation research is—What is the relationship between two or more variables for a given set of subjects. Notice that we said relationship between variables and not the effect of one variable on another variable.

In descriptive research we are just describing our subjects in terms of one or more variables, while in correlational research we are looking at the relationship between the variables.

For correlational research we are just looking at the degree of relationship between the variables and not the effect of one variable on another variable. One important type of correlational research are studies conducted to provide information about the validity and reliability of tests.

Reliability studies are conducted to demonstrate the consistency with which tests perform their measurement function. In one type of reliability study the same group of subjects is given a test and then at a somewhat later date are given the test again. We thus have two scores for each subject (the test score and the retest score) and the correlation coefficient between the two sets of scores can be calculated.

The reliability coefficient can also be calculated by using equivalent forms of the test. Many tests used in education, for example, standardised achievement tests, have more than one form. To determine the reliability coefficient, a group of subjects are given both forms of a test thus two scores are obtained for each subject and the correlation coefficient is calculated for the two sets of scores.

The first type of correlation study we referred to is a test-retest reliability study and the second is an equivalent forms reliability study.

To demonstrate the validity of a test we want to show that scores on the test correlate highly with some external measure of what the test purportedly measures. This external measure is referred to as the criterion to conduct a validity correlational study. We obtain scores for students on some test and also record their scores on the criterion measure. Thus we have two scores for each subject and can calculate the correlation coefficient of the sets of scores. This correlation coefficient is referred to as a validity coefficient.

In the follow are some of the tests that might be used in validity studies.

i) Reading Comprehension

ii) Jiffy IQ Test

iii) Clinical Depression Scale

iv) Algebra Prediction Test

8.8.1. Characteristics of Correlation

Correlational research studies almost always use the correlation coefficient to indicate the degree of relationship between two variables. The correlation coefficient is a number ranging from 1 (a perfect positive correlation) through 0 (no relationship between the variables) to -1 (a perfect negative correlation).

A correlation coefficient is indicating the proportion of sameness between the two variables. A correlation of .90 does not mean that the two variables are 90% the same. In fact, the proportion of common variance (an indication of sameness) for a correlation of .90 is .81 or 81%. The proportion of common variance is the square of the correlation coefficient. (.90 x .90 = .8100).

8.8.2. Design of Correlational Research

8.8.2.1. Prediction Studies

In predictive correlational studies we are using the degree of relationship that exists between two variables to predict one variable from the other. For example if reading and spelling are correlated, then we can use the information to predict a student's score on the spelling test if the student has only taken the reading test. Conversely we could predict the student's score on the reading test given the student's score on the spelling test. Prediction studies are widely used to predict student academic success in college based on such measures as high school grades, teacher grades, and aptitude test scores. In fact, many such criteria may be used in a multiple correlation prediction study.

8.9. Causal-Comparative Research

Causal-comparative educational research attempts to identify a causative relationship between an independent variable and a dependent variable. However, this relationship is more suggestive than proven as the researcher does not have complete control over the independent variable. If the researcher had control over the independent variable, then the research would be classified as true experimental research.

There are many occasions while conducting educational research during which the researcher is unable to control the independent variable, or it would be unethical to control the independent variable, or it is simply too difficult to control the independent variable. For example, someone attempting to find the effect of gender (male or female) on an educational dependent variable would not be able to experimentally manipulate gender, and thus would use a causal-comparative research design rather than an experimental design for the research.

The statement or title of a causal-comparative research study takes the form: The effect of [independent variable] on [dependent variable] for [subjects], with the understanding that the independent variable is not under experimental control. An important difference between causal-comparative and correlational research is that causal-comparative studies involve two or more groups and one independent variable, while correlational studies involve two or more variables and one group.

8.9.1. Nature of Causal-Comparative Research

The basic design of a causal-comparative research study is to select a group that has the independent variable (the experimental group) and then select another group of subjects that does not have the independent variable (the control or comparison group). The two groups are then compared on the dependent variable. For example, in your junior high school, some of the seventh grade math classes use hand held calculators in their seventh grade mathematics classes, while other classes do not use calculators. You want to find the effect of calculator use on mathematics grades at the end of the year. So you select a group of students from the classes that use calculators and then select another group of the same size from the classes that do not use calculators and compare the two groups at the end of the year on their final math grades. Another variant of this study would be to take the students from one class that uses calculators and compare them with another class that does not use calculators. Both these studies would be causal-comparative research studies but they would differ in how you can generalise the results of your study. The results of the first study could be generalised to the seventh grade students taking mathematics classes in your school while the second study could only be generalised to the two classes that participated in the study.

One of the problems with causal-comparative research is that since the pupils are not randomly placed in the groups, the groups can differ on other variables that may have an effect on the

dependent variable. In experimental research we can assume that these other variables cancel out among the study groups by the process of randomisation. However, in causal-comparative research if we are suspicious that some external variable might be involved, we can use some control procedure in an attempt to ameliorate the effect of the external variable.

8.9.2. Methods for Causal-Comparative Studies

8.9.2.1 Matching

It is one way to help control the effect of extraneous variables on the dependent variable in a causal-comparative study. For example, let's say you do not think that the two groups that you are using to evaluate a new approach to reading instruction are similar on verbal ability. Further you suspect that verbal ability might be related to the dependent variable in this study. The dependent variable is performance on a reading test. To overcome this difficulty you assess each of your students with a measure of verbal ability, such as a test of general intelligence, and then select pairs of subjects, one from each group, that are similar to each other in verbal abilily.

In this causal-comparative study, the independent variable is method for reading instruction. The dependent variable, is reading proficiency, and verbal ability is the matching or control variable. Another method to control the effect of an extraneous variable on the dependent variable is to compare homogeneous subgroups. This would constrict the number of subjects we could use in our study, but would help control the effect of tested intelligence (verbal ability) on the dependent variable in the study.

A third method that is sometimes used to control the effects of an extraneous variable is analysis of covariance. Analysis of covariance is a statistical method of control in which the scores on the dependent variable are adjusted for the subject's initial differences in the control variable.

8.9.2.2 Analysis of Data

An inferential statistic used in both causal-comparative and experimental research designs is the t-test. Where the subjects in the two groups are independent of one another, that is no matching of subjects or other control procedures were used, the independent t-test is used to test the significance of a difference between the means of the experimental and control groups in the study.

In research designs where the influence of an extraneous variable has been controlled, or in designs utilising a pre-test-post-test procedure, the appropriate t-test to use to compare the two groups would be the dependent t-test. When you have three or more groups to compare, the appropriate inferential statistic to use would be one-way analysis of variance. This statistic shows the significance of differences in the means of three or more groups of subjects.

In cases where you are using frequency counts for the dependent variable, the appropriate inferential statistic to use would be the chi-square test. This statistic tests the significance of differences between two or more groups (independent variable) in frequencies for the dependent variable.

8.10. Experimental Research

There are different types of experiments. Most of them are quite different from the common stereotype. All experimental research, however, has several elements in common. One of the most obvious is the division of the subjects into groups (control, experimental, etc). Another is the use of a "treatment" (usually the independent variable) which is introduced into the research context or manipulated by the researcher. The four research parameters (discussed earlier in this module) will help us understand the other distinguishing characteristics of experimental research.

The major difference between causal-comparative and experimental research is that the researcher has control over the independent variable in experimental research and can manipulate this variable at will. In the case of causal-comparative research, the independent variable is established by the identity of the groups chosen and is not under experimental control. For the variable, gender, we can't randomly assign the values of male and female to our subjects, they are predetermined. So a study attempting to determine the relationship between gender and some independent variable would be a causal-comparative

research design. On the other hand, a study attempting to describe the relationship between the use or non-use of coloured overlays on the frequency of oral reading errors would be an experimental study if the subjects were randomly placed in the experimental and control groups.

If you choose to conduct experimental research, one of your most important tasks will be to choose the design that gives your research the best combination of internal and external validity. At the same time, it must be practical enough so that you can actually do the research in your own circumstances.

No particular type is right for all situations. Real-world constraints will often dictate what is practical or possible. In any case you need to be careful to recognise the weaknesses of the design you choose. Do not attempt to prove things or make claims in your findings that are beyond the capabilities of your design.

8.10.1. General Approach

On the synthetic-analytic continuum, experimental research tends to fall on the analytic end. Unless it is very complicated, an experiment typically focuses on a specific element (a "constituent part") of the larger process of language learning and teaching.

8.10.2. Research Aim

The next parameter deals with the heuristic (hypothesis-generating) vs. deductive (hypothesis-testing) factor. In contrast to qualitative research, virtually all experiments are designed to test hypotheses.

8.10.3. Control Over The Research Context

Experiments generally fall on the high end of this scale because they attempt to control the research environment to a considerable degree. This can be both a plus and a minus.

On the one hand, it allows the researcher to isolate a particular variable and focus on it in order to determine its effect on other variables. Because of this feature, only experimental studies can claim to show any degree of causality. Qualitative and descriptive research can reveal only relationships or processes.

On the other hand, control has several disadvantages. One is that it often makes the research situation unnatural. Consequently, subjects may not behave normally in an experiment. Another disadvantage is that it is virtually impossible to control all the variables in a research situation involving human beings. Finally, controlled experiments often raise serious questions about research ethics.

8.10.4. Explicitness of Data Collection Procedures

The final parameter deals with the level of explicitness in data collection. Here again, experimental research falls toward the high end of the scale. Carefully focused instruments (tests, observations, questionnaires, etc.) that generate precise quantitative data are the norm in experiments. These data can be analysed using statistical tests of significance in order to accept or reject the hypothesis.

8.10.5. Group Experimental Designs

Within the realm of experimental research, there are three major types of design:

— Pre-Experimental Designs
- a) The One-Shot Case Study
- b) The One-Group Pretest-Post-test Design
- c) The Static-Group Comparison

— True Experimental Designs
- a) The Pretest-Post-test Control Group Design
- b) The Post-test-Only Control Group Design
- c) The Solomon Four-Group Design

— Quasi-Experimental Designs
- a) The Nonequivalent Control Group design
- b) The Time-Series Design

— Counterbalanced Designs

8.10.6. True-Experimental Designs

Random selection of subjects

— Use of control groups
— Random assignments to control and experimental groups
— Random assignment of groups to control and experimental conditions

In order for an experiment to follow a true-experimental design, it must meet the preceding criteria. There is some variation in true-experimental designs, but that variation comes in the time(s) that the treatment is given to the experimental group, or in the observation or measurement (pre-test, post-test, mid-test) area.

8.10.7. Quasi-Experimental Designs

These are usually constructions that already exist in the real world. Those designs that fall into the quasi-experimental category fall short in some way of the criteria for the true experimental group. A quasi-experimental design will have some sort of control and experimental group, but these groups probably weren't randomly selected. Random selection is usually where true-experimental and quasi-experimental designs differ.

8.10.8. Pre-Experimental Designs

These are lacking in several areas of the true-experimental criteria. Not only do they lack random selection in most cases, but they usually just employ a single group. This group receives the "treatment," there is no control group. Pilot studies, one-shot case studies, and most research using only one group, fall into this category.

8.11. Conclusion

Research is a method used for finding out the truth unknown. A researcher can choose any method according to his/her choice to unearth these facts. The credibility of a research depends on the integrity of a person who conducts the research. A careless study will besmirch the entire research work. So the researcher must be extra careful while going through each and every step of a research process.

REFERENCES

Berg, B.L., *Qualitative Research Methods for the Social Science*, Allyn and Bacon, 1989.

Borg, W.R., and Gall, M.D., *Educational Research: An Introduction*, (Fifth edition) Longman, 1989.

Bulmer, M., *Sociological Research Methods*, (Second edition) Macmillan, 1984.

Cohen, L., and Manion, I., *Research Methods in Education*, 1989.

Dominowski, R.L., *Research Methods*, Prentice-Hall, 1980.

Ely, M., Anzul, M., Friedman, T., Garner, D., and Steinmetz, A.M., *Doing Qualitative Research: Circles within Circles*, Falmer Press, 1990.

Falmer Press McNeill, P., *Research Methods*, (Second edition) Routledge, 1990.

Isaac, S., and Michael, W.B., *Handbook in Research and Evaluation for Education and the Behavioural Sciences*, EdITS Publishers, 1989.

Routledge. Denzin, N.K., and Lincoln, Y.S. (Eds.) *Handbook of Qualitative Research*, Sage, 1994.

9

Techniques of Data Collection

9.1. Introduction

Data are a collection of information, evidence, or facts from which you can draw conclusions. Collection of data means the gathering of information. There are various methods of data collection such as personal interviewing, telephone, mail and the Internet. Depending on the survey design, these methods can be used separately or combined. Although deciding on data collection tools and methods and actually collecting data are actually two different steps in the evaluation cycle.

— Data can be quantitative—numeric information—or it can be qualitative—involving stories, observations, etc.

— Data are important because they offer evidence for the outcomes your programme is producing and allow you to confidently make the case for your programmes. The data that you want to collect will be driven from the questions you want answered.

There are a variety of different types of data collection methods. You can also use alternative documentation approaches including having programme participants keep written, audio, or video journals of both their experiences and their thoughts, feelings, etc. Data collection can be implemented after:

i) Finalise your evaluation questions.

ii) Decide what information you already have and what information you will need to collect.

iii) Based on the type of data you need, choose an appropriate data collection method.

iv) Develop tools to collect the data.

While it is impossible to collect data without any bias, it is possible to minimise bias. You can do this by gathering as many perspectives as possible, using a variety of methods, checking your interpretations with the programme stakeholders, and ensuring that data collectors aren't biasing responses by asking leading questions or incentivising the respondent to answer in a particular way.

Once you have chosen your data collection method(s) you are ready to collect the data. The following are some guidelines for collecting data:

1. No matter what type of data collection tools you decide to use, you should test them with a small sample of volunteers before you implement data collection. This will allow you to determine whether the tools are easy to understand, whether the questions are clear, relevant, and unbiased, if the data collection could be completed in a reasonable amount of time, and whether there are any improvements that could be made to the data collection tool.
2. Establish a firm schedule for data collection.
3. Ensure the data collectors have both the training and the tools they need for collecting data.
4. Make sure data is carefully stored and that confidentiality is maintained. This does not mean that you can not report the data, but rather that you do not associate any of the data with a particular person.

9.2. Primary Data Collection Methods

In primary data collection, you collect the data yourself using methods such as interviews and questionnaires. The key point here is that the data you collect is unique to you and your research and, until you publish, no one else has access to it. There are many methods of collecting primary data and the main methods include:

— Questionnaires

— Interviews

— Focus group interviews

— Observation

— Case-studies
— Diaries
— Critical incidents
— Portfolios

The primary data, which is generated by the above methods, may be qualitative in nature (usually in the form of words) or quantitative (usually in the form of numbers or where you can make counts of words used).

9.2.1. Questionnaires

Questionnaires are a popular means of collecting data, but are difficult to design and often require many rewrites before an acceptable questionnaire is produced.

Advantages

— Can be used as a method in its own right or as a basis for interviewing or a telephone survey.
— Can be posted, e-mailed or faxed.
— Can cover a large number of people or organisations.
— Wide geographic coverage.
— Relatively cheap.
— No prior arrangements are needed.
— Avoids embarrassment on the part of the respondent.
— Respondent can consider responses.
— Possible anonymity of respondent.
— No interviewer bias.

Disadvantages

— Design problems.
— Questions have to be relatively simple.
— Historically low response rate (although inducements may help).
— Time delay whilst waiting for responses to be returned.
— Require a return deadline.

— Several reminders may be required.
— Assumes no literacy problems.
— No control over who completes it.
— Not possible to give assistance if required.
— Problems with incomplete questionnaires.
— Replies not spontaneous and independent of each other.
— Respondent can read all questions beforehand and then decide whether to complete or not. For example, perhaps because it is too long, too complex, uninteresting, or too personal.

9.2.1.1. Essentials of Postal Questionnaires

Covering Letter: The general theme of the questionnaire should be made explicit in a covering letter. You should state who you are; why the data is required; give, if necessary, an assurance of confidentiality and/or anonymity; and contact number and address or telephone number. This ensures that the respondents know what they are committing themselves to, and also that they understand the context of their replies. If possible, you should offer an estimate of the completion time. Instructions for return should be included with the return date made obvious.

Request of Completion: You need to provide clear and unambiguous instructions for completion. Within most questionnaires these are general instructions and specific instructions for particular question structures. It is usually best to separate these, supplying the general instructions as a preamble to the questionnaire, but leaving the specific instructions until the questions to which they apply. The response method should be indicated (circle, tick, cross, etc). Wherever possible, and certainly if a slightly unfamiliar response system is employed, you should give an example.

Appearance: Appearance is usually the first feature of the questionnaire to which the recipient reacts. A neat and professional look will encourage further consideration of your request, increasing your response rate. In addition, careful thought to layout should help your analysis. There are a number of simple rules to help improve questionnaire appearance:

— Liberal spacing makes the reading easier.

— Photo-reduction can produce more space without reducing content.

— Consistent positioning of response boxes, usually to the right, speeds up completion and also avoids inadvertent omission of responses.

— Choose the font style to maximise legibility.

— Differentiate between instructions and questions. Either lower case or capitals can be used, or responses can be boxed.

Length: Excessive size can only reduce response rates. If a long questionnaire is necessary, then you must give even more thought to appearance. It is best to leave pages unnumbered.

Order: Probably the most crucial stage in questionnaire response is the beginning. Once the respondents have started to complete the questions they will normally finish the task, unless it is very long or difficult. Consequently, you need to select the opening questions with care. Usually the best approach is to ask for biographical details first, as the respondents should know all the answers without much thought. Another benefit is that an easy start provides practice in answering questions.

Once the introduction has been achieved the subsequent order will depend on many considerations. You should be aware of the varying importance of different questions. Essential information should appear early, just in case the questionnaire is not completed. For the same reasons, relatively unimportant questions can be placed towards the end. If questions are likely to provoke the respondent and remain unanswered, these too are best left until the end, in the hope of obtaining answers to everything else.

Coding: If analysis of the results is to be carried out using a statistical package or spreadsheet it is advisable to code non-numerical responses when designing the questionnaire, rather than trying to code the responses when they are returned.

Thank you: Respondents to questionnaires rarely benefit personally from their efforts and the least the researcher can do is to thank them. Even though the covering letter will express appreciation for the help given, it is also a nice gesture to finish the questionnaire with a further thank you.

9.2.1.2 *Preparation of Questions*

— Keep the questions short, simple and to the point; avoid all unnecessary words.

— Use words and phrases that are unambiguous and familiar to the respondent.

— Only ask questions that the respondent can answer. Hypothetical questions should be avoided. Avoid calculations and questions that require a lot of memory work.

— Avoid loaded or leading questions that imply a certain answer.

— Vacuous words or phrases should be avoided. 'Generally', 'usually', or 'normally' are imprecise terms with various meanings. They should be replaced with quantitative statements, for example, 'at least once a week'.

— Questions should only address a single issue.

— Do not ask two questions in one by using 'and'.

— Avoid double negatives. Respondents may tackle a double negative by switching both negatives and then assuming that the same answer applies. This is not necessarily valid.

— State units required but do not aim for too high a degree of accuracy.

9.2.1.3. *Types of Questions*

Closed Questions: A question is asked and then a number of possible answers are provided for the respondent. The respondent selects the answer which is appropriate. Closed questions are particularly useful in obtaining factual information.

Attitude Questions: Frequently questions are asked to find out the respondents' opinions or attitudes to a given situation. A Likert scale provides a battery of attitude statements. The respondent then says how much they agree or disagree with each one.

A semantic differential scale attempts to see how strongly an attitude is held by the respondent. With these scales double-ended terms are given to the respondents who are asked to indicate where their attitude lies on the scale between the terms. The response can be indicated by putting a cross in a particular position or circling a number.

Open Questions: An open question such as 'What are the essential skills a manager should possess?' should be used as an adjunct to the main theme of the questionnaire and could allow the respondent to elaborate upon an earlier more specific question. Open questions inserted at the end of major sections, or at the end of the questionnaire, can act as safety valves, and possibly offer additional information. However, they should not be used to introduce a section since there is a high risk of influencing later responses. The main problem of open questions is that many different answers have to be summarised and possibly coded.

9.2.1.4. Testing

Questionnaire design is fraught with difficulties and problems. A number of rewrites will be necessary, together with refinement and rethinks on a regular basis. Do not assume that you will write the questionnaire accurately and perfectly at the first attempt. If poorly designed, you will collect inappropriate or inaccurate data and good analysis cannot then rectify the situation.

To refine the questionnaire, you need to conduct a pilot survey. This is a small-scale trial prior to the main survey that tests all your question planning. Amendments to questions can be made. After making some amendments, the new version would be re-tested. If this re-test produces more changes, another pilot would be undertaken and so on. For example, perhaps responses to open-ended questions become closed; questions which are all answered the same way can be omitted; difficult words replaced, etc.

It is usual to pilot the questionnaires personally so that the respondent can be observed and questioned if necessary. By timing each question, you can identify any questions that appear too difficult, and you can also obtain a reliable estimate of the anticipated completion time for inclusion in the covering letter.

The result can also be use to test the coding and analytical procedures to be performed later.

9.2.1.5. Distribution and Return

The questionnaire should be checked for completeness to ensure that all pages are present and that none is blank or illegible. It is usual to supply a prepaid addressed envelope for the return of the questionnaire. You need to explain this in the covering letter and reinforce it at the end of the questionnaire, after the 'Thank you'.

Finally, many organisations are approached continually for information. Many, as a matter of course, will not respond in a positive way.

9.2.2. Interviews

Interviewing is a technique that is primarily used to gain an understanding of the underlying reasons and motivations for people's attitudes, preferences or behaviour. Interviews can be undertaken on a personal one-to-one basis or in a group. They can be conducted at work, at home, in the street or in a shopping centre, or some other agreed location.

9.2.2.1. Types of Interviews

Personal Interviews:

Advantages

- — Serious approach by respondent resulting in accurate information.
- — Good response rate.
- — Completed and immediate.
- — Possible in-depth questions.
- — Interviewer in control and can give help if there is a problem.
- — Can investigate motives and feelings.
- — Can use recording equipment.
- — Characteristics of respondent assessed—tone of voice, facial expression, hesitation, etc.

— Can use props.
— If one interviewer used, uniformity of approach.
— Used to pilot other methods.

Disadvantages

— Need to set up interviews.
— Time consuming.
— Geographic limitations.
— Can be expensive.
— Normally need a set of questions.
— Respondent bias—tendency to please or impress, create false personal image, or end interview quickly.
— Embarrassment possible if personal questions.
— Transcription and analysis can present problems—subjectivity.

Structured Interview

— Based on a carefully worded interview schedule.
— Frequently require short answers with the answers being ticked off.
— Useful when there are a lot of questions which are not particularly contentious or thought provoking.
— Respondent may become irritated by having to give over-simplified answers.

Semi-structured: The interview is focused by asking certain questions but with scope for the respondent to express him or herself at length.

Unstructured: This also called an in-depth interview. The interviewer begins by asking a general question. The interviewer then encourages the respondent to talk freely. The interviewer uses an unstructured format, the subsequent direction of the interview being determined by the respondent's initial reply. The interviewer then probes for elaboration.

Telephone Interview

This is an alternative form of interview to the personal, face-to-face interview.

Advantages

— Relatively cheap.

— Quick.

— Can cover reasonably large numbers of people or organisations.

— Wide geographic coverage.

— High response rate—keep going till the required number.

— No waiting.

— Spontaneous response.

— Can tape answers.

Disadvantages

— Often connected with selling.

— Questionnaire required.

— Not everyone has a telephone.

— Repeat calls are inevitable—average 2.5 calls to get someone.

— Time is wasted.

— Straightforward questions are required.

— Respondent has little time to think.

— Cannot use visual aids.

— Can cause irritation.

— Good telephone manner is required.

— Question of authority.

Planning an Interview

— List the areas in which you require information.

— Decide on type of interview.

— Transform areas into actual questions.

— Try them out on a friend or relative.

— Make an appointment with respondent(s)—discussing details of why and how long.

— Try and fix a venue and time when you will not be disturbed

Focus Group Interviews

A focus group is an interview conducted by a trained moderator in a non-structured and natural manner with a small group of respondents. The moderator leads the discussion. The main purpose of focus groups is to gain insights by listening to a group of people from the appropriate target market talk about specific issues of interest.

9.2.4. Observation

Observation involves recording the behavioural patterns of people, objects and events in a systematic manner. Observational methods may be:

- — structured or unstructured
- — disguised or undisguised
- — natural or contrived
- — personal
- — mechanical
- — non-participant
- — participant, with the participant taking a number of different roles

9.2.4.1. Structured or Unstructured

In structured observation, the researcher specifies in detail what is to be observed and how the measurements are to be recorded. It is appropriate when the problem is clearly defined and the information needed is specified.

In unstructured observation, the researcher monitors all aspects of the phenomenon that seem relevant. It is appropriate when the problem has yet to be formulated precisely and flexibility is needed in observation to identify key components of the problem and to develop hypotheses. The potential for bias is high. Observation findings should be treated as hypotheses to be tested rather than as conclusive findings.

9.2.4.2. Disguised or Undisguised

In disguised observation, respondents are unaware they are being observed and thus behave naturally. Disguise is achieved, for example, by hiding, or using hidden equipment or people disguised as shoppers.

In undisguised observation, respondents are aware they are being observed. There is a danger of the Hawthorne effect — people behave differently when being observed.

9.2.4.3. *Natural or Contrived*

Natural observation involves observing behaviour as it takes place in the environment, for example, eating hamburgers in a fast food outlet.

In contrived observation, the respondents' behaviour is observed in an artificial environment, for example, a food tasting session.

9.2.4.4. *Personal*

In personal observation, a researcher observes actual behaviour as it occurs. The observer may or may not normally attempt to control or manipulate the phenomenon being observed. The observer merely records what takes place.

9.2.4.5. *Mechanical*

Mechanical devices (video, closed circuit television) record what is being observed. These devices may or may not require the respondent's direct participation. They are used for continuously recording on-going behaviour.

9.2.4.6. *Non-participant*

The observer does not normally question or communicate with the people being observed. He or she does not participate.

9.2.4.7. *Participant*

In participant observation, the researcher becomes, or is, part of the group that is being investigated. Participant observation has its roots in ethnographic studies (study of man and races) where researchers would live in tribal villages, attempting to understand the customs and practices of that culture. It has a very extensive literature, particularly in sociology (development, nature and laws of human society) and anthropology (physiological and psychological study of man). Organisations can be viewed as 'tribes' with their own customs and practices.

The role of the participant observer is not simple. There are different ways of classifying the role:

— Researcher as employee.
— Researcher as an explicit role.
— Interrupted involvement.
— Observation alone.

Researcher as Employee: The researcher works within the organisation alongside other employees, effectively as one of them. The role of the researcher may or may not be explicit and this will have implications for the extent to which he or she will be able to move around and gather information and perspectives from other sources. This role is appropriate when the researcher needs to become totally immersed and experience the work or situation at first hand.

Researcher as an Explicit Role: The researcher is present every day over a period of time, but entry is negotiated in advance with management and preferably with employees as well. The individual is quite clearly in the role of a researcher who can move around, observe, interview and participate in the work as appropriate. This type of role is the most favoured, as it provides many of the insights that the complete observer would gain, whilst offering much greater flexibility without the ethical problems that deception entails.

Interrupted Involvement: The researcher is present sporadically over a period of time, for example, moving in and out of the organisation to deal with other work or to conduct interviews with, or observations of, different people across a number of different organisations. It rarely involves much participation in the work.

Observation Alone: The observer role is often disliked by employees since it appears to be 'eavesdropping'. The inevitable detachment prevents the degree of trust and friendship forming between the researcher and respondent, which is an important component in other methods.

9.2.5. Case-studies

The term case-study usually refers to a fairly intensive examination of a single unit such as a person, a small group of people, or a single company. Case-studies involve measuring what is there and how it got there. In this sense, it is historical. It can enable the researcher to explore, unravel and understand problems, issues and relationships. It cannot, however, allow the researcher to generalise, that is, to argue that from one case-study the results, findings or theory developed apply to other similar case-studies. The case looked at may be unique and, therefore not representative of other instances. It is, of course, possible to look at several case-studies to represent certain features of management that we are interested in studying. The case-study approach is often done to make practical improvements. Contributions to general knowledge are incidental. The case-study method has four steps:

1. Determine the present situation.
2. Gather background information about the past and key variables.
3. Test hypotheses. The background information collected will have been analysed for possible hypotheses. In this step, specific evidence about each hypothesis can be gathered. This step aims to eliminate possibilities which conflict with the evidence collected and to gain confidence for the important hypotheses. The culmination of this step might be the development of an experimental design to test out more rigorously the hypotheses developed, or it might be to take action to remedy the problem.
4. Take remedial action. The aim is to check that the hypotheses tested actually work out in practice. Some action, correction or improvement is made and a re-check carried out on the situation to see what effect the change has brought about.

The case-study enables rich information to be gathered from which potentially useful hypotheses can be generated. It can be a time-consuming process. It is also inefficient in researching situations which are already well structured and where the important variables have been identified. They lack utility when attempting to reach rigorous conclusions or determining precise relationships between variables.

9.2.6. Diaries

A diary is a way of gathering information about the way individuals spend their time on professional activities. Diaries can record either quantitative or qualitative data, and in management research can provide information about work patterns and activities.

9.2.7. Critical Incidents

The critical incident technique is an attempt to identify the more 'noteworthy' aspects of job behaviour and is based on the assumption that jobs are composed of critical and non-critical tasks. For example, a critical task might be defined as one that makes the difference between success and failure in carrying out important parts of the job. The idea is to collect reports about what people do that is particularly effective in contributing to good performance. The incidents are scaled in order of difficulty, frequency and importance to the job as a whole.

The technique scores over the use of diaries as it is centred on specific happenings and on what is judged as effective behaviour. However, it is laborious and does not lend itself to objective quantification.

9.2.8. Portfolios

A measure of a manager's ability may be expressed in terms of the number and duration of 'issues' or problems being tackled at any one time. The compilation of problem portfolios is recording information about how each problem arose, methods used to solve it, difficulties encountered, etc. This analysis also raises questions about the person's use of time. What proportion of time is occupied in checking; in handling problems given by others; on self-generated problems; on 'top-priority' problems; on minor issues, etc? The main problem with this method and the use of diaries is getting people to agree to record everything in sufficient detail for you to analyse. It is very time-consuming.

9.2.9. Sampling

Collecting data is time consuming and expensive, even for relatively small amounts of data. Hence, it is highly unlikely that a complete population will be investigated. Because of the time and cost elements the amount of data you collect will be limited and the number of people or organisations you contact will be small in number. You will, therefore, have to take a sample and usually a small sample.

Sampling theory says a correctly taken sample of an appropriate size will yield results that can be applied to the population as a whole.

9.2.9.1. Simple random sampling

Simple random sampling can be carried out in two ways—the lottery method and using random numbers. This is basically similar to a game of bingo or the national lottery. This procedure is easy to carry out especially if both population and sample are small, but can be tedious and time consuming for large populations or large samples. Alternatively random numbers can be used. Random numbers are strings of digits that have been generated by the lottery method and can be found in books of statistical tables.

9.2.10. Data Recording and Analysis

Data analysis is the process of bringing order, structure and meaning to the mass of collected data. It is a messy, ambiguous, time-consuming, creative, and fascinating process. It does not proceed in a linear fashion; it is not neat. Qualitative data analysis is a search for general statements about relationships among categories of data. When you are at the planning stage of your research design, it is worth thinking about how you are going to record your data and, even more importantly, how you are going to analyse it. It is pointless collecting data in a form that you cannot understand or analyse.

9.3. Secondary Data Collection Methods

All methods of data collection can supply quantitative data (numbers, statistics or financial) or qualitative data (usually words or text). Quantitative data may often be presented in tabular or graphical form. Secondary data is data that has already been collected by someone else for a different purpose to yours.

Most research requires the collection of primary data (data that you collect at first hand), and this is what students concentrate on. Unfortunately, many dissertations do not include secondary data in their findings section although it is perfectly acceptable to do so, providing you have analysed it. It is always a good idea to use data collected by someone else if it exists—it may be on a much larger scale than you could hope to collect and could contribute to your findings considerably.

There are many sources of data and most people tend to underestimate the number of sources and the amount of data within each of these sources. Sources can be classified as:

— paper-based sources—books, journals, periodicals, abstracts, indexes, directories, research reports, conference papers, market reports, annual reports, internal records of organisations, newspapers and magazines

— electronic sources- CD-ROMs, on-line databases, Internet, videos and broadcasts.

The main sources of qualitative and quantitative secondary data include:

— Official or government sources.

— Unofficial or general business sources.

— European Union (Community) sources.

— International sources.

9.4. Purpose of Data Analysis

The purpose of analysing data is to obtain usable and useful information. The analysis, irrespective of whether the data is qualitative or quantitative.

A misconception, and source of confusion for many people, is the belief that qualitative research generates just qualitative data (text, words, opinions, etc) and that quantitative research generates just quantitative data (numbers). Sometimes this is the case, but both types of data can be generated by each approach.

A second misconception is that statistical techniques are only applicable for quantitative data. Once again, this is not so. There are many statistical techniques that can be applied to qualitative data, such as ratings scales, that has been generated by a quantitative research approach. Many people are worried about numbers, and in particular about statistics, and everything that word implies. Quantitative research and the analysis of quantitative data is consequently something to be avoided. But as we have indicated above, this is rarely possible because qualitative data can also be analysed using statistics. An understanding of basic statistical terms and ideas and the ability to carry out some statistical analysis (elementary or otherwise) is essential for most researchers. Also competence in these techniques, even at a basic level, is a useful skill in its own right.

A third misconception is that qualitative data analysis is easy. There are many ways of conducting qualitative research and thus many ways of analysing the resulting (qualitative) data. For example, having conducted an interview, transcription and organisation of data are the first stages of analysis. This would then be continued by systematically analysing the transcripts, grouping together comments on similar themes and attempting to interpret them and draw conclusions. Data that can be analysed statistically (quantitative data and some types of qualitative data) in the section called quantitative data analysis. We cover data that cannot, or is very difficult, to analyse statistically in the section called qualitative data analysis.

9.5. Qualitative Data Analysis

Qualitative data is subjective, rich, and in-depth information normally presented in the form of words. In undergraduate dissertations, the most common form of qualitative data is derived from semi-structured or unstructured interviews, although other sources can include observations, life histories and journals and documents of all kinds including newspapers.

Qualitative data from interviews can be analysed for content (content analysis) or for the language used (discourse analysis). Qualitative data is difficult to analyse and often opportunities to achieve high marks are lost because the data is treated casually and without rigour. Here we concentrate on the content analysis of data from interviews.

9.5.1. Theory

When using a quantitative methodology, you are normally testing theory through the testing of a hypothesis. In qualitative research, you are either exploring the application of a theory or model in a different context or are hoping for a theory or a model to emerge from the data. In other words, although you may have some ideas about your topic, you are also looking for ideas, concepts and attitudes often from experts or practitioners in the field.

9.5.2. Collecting and Organising Data

The means of collecting and recording data through interviews and the possible pitfalls are well documented elsewhere but in terms of subsequent analysis, it is essential that you have a complete and accurate record of what was said. Do not rely on your memory and either tape record the conversation (preferably) or take copious notes. If you are taking notes, write them up straight after the interview so that you can elaborate and clarify. If you are using a tape recorder, transcribe the exact words onto paper.

However you record the data, you should end up with a hard copy of either exactly what was said (transcript of tape recording) or nearly exactly what was said (comprehensive notes). It may be that parts of the interview are irrelevant or are more in the nature of background material, in which case you need not put these into your transcript but do make sure that they are indeed unnecessary. You should indicate omissions in the text with short statements.

9.5.3. Content Analysis

Analysis of qualitative data is not simple, and although it does not require complicated statistical techniques of quantitative analysis, it is nonetheless difficult to handle the usually large amounts of data in a thorough, systematic and relevant manner.

9.5.4. Coding Paragraphs

This is where you mark each paragraph with a topic/theme/category with an appropriate word in the margin.

9.5.5 Presentation of Qualitative Data

This would normally follow the topics, themes and categories that you have developed in the analysis and these, in turn, are likely to have been themes that came out in the literature and may have formed the basis for your interview questions. It is usually a mistake to go through each interviewee in turn and what they said on each topic. This is cumbersome and does not give the scope to compare and contrast their ideas with the ideas of others.

Do not analyse the data on a question-by-question basis. You should summarise the key themes that emerge from the data and may give selected quotes if these are particularly appropriate.

9.6. Quantitative Data Analysis

Here we are concerned with the basics of statistical analysis. However, we do not cover the techniques in detail but provide a brief overview. If you are unsure of these or have forgotten them, you should refer to your notes from previous studies or consult introductory statistics textbooks. We begin by looking at some basic ideas about analysis and presentation of data. These are 'variables' and the related idea of 'scales of measurement'.

9.6.1. Variables

Constant reference is made in statistics textbooks to the term variable. A variable is a characteristic of interest that varies from one item to another and may take any one of a specified set of values or attributes. Variables are usually classified as quantitative or qualitative. For example, consider a study of guests at a hotel. We may be interested in the age of a guest, their spend and length of stay. Each characteristic is a quantitative variable because the data that each generates is numerical. Quantitative variables generate quantitative data. On the other hand, qualitative variables generate non-numerical or qualitative data.

9.6.2. Scales of Measurement

Many people are confused about what type of analysis to use on a set of data and the relevant forms of pictorial presentation or data display. The decision is based on the scale of measurement of the data. These scales are nominal, ordinal and numerical.

A nominal scale is where the data can be classified into a non-numerical or named categories, and the order in which these categories can be written or asked is arbitrary. An ordinal scale is where the data can be classified into non-numerical or named categories.

A numerical scale is where numbers represent the possible response categories. There is a natural ranking of the categories and zero on the scale has meaning. There is a quantifiable difference within categories and between consecutive categories.

Content analysis consists of reading and re-reading the transcripts looking for similarities and differences in order to find themes and to develop categories. Having the full transcript is essential to make sure that you do not leave out anything of importance by only selecting material that fits your own ideas.

9.7. Conclusion

Each and every process of research is vital, but the collection of data and its analysis is the backbone of a research. Data or information can be collected in many ways. Data collection is prone to biases and is easy to get wrong information. So the researcher should ensure its authenticity.

References

Dey, I., *Qualitative data analysis: A user-friendly guide for social scientists,* New York: Routledge, 1993.

Kelle, U. (Ed.), *Computer-aided qualitative data analysis,* Thousand Oaks, CA: SAGE, 1995.

Kirchhoff, K. T., "Design of questionnaires and structured interviews", In M. A. Mateo & K. T. Kirchhoff (Eds.), *Using and conducting nursing research in the clinical setting,* Philadelphia: Saunders, 1999.

Knafl, K.A., & Webster, D.C., "Managing and analyzing qualitative data: A description of tasks, techniques, and materials", *Western Journal of Nursing Research,* 1988.

May, K.A., "Interview techniques in qualitative research: Concerns and challenges", In J.M. Morse (Ed.), *Qualitative nursing research: A contemporary dialogue,* Newbury Park, CA: Sage, 1991.

Maxwell, J. A., "Understanding and validity in qualitative research", *Harvard Educational Review,* 1992.

Morse, J.M., "Emerging from the data": The cognitive processes of analysis in qualitative inquiry, In J. M. Morse (Ed.), *Critical issues in qualitative research methods*, Thousand Oaks, CA: Sage, 1994.

Newman I., *Qualitative-Quantitative Research Methodology: Exploring the Interactive Continuum*, Carbondale: Southern Illinois University Press, 1998.

Williamson K., *Research Methods for Students and Professionals: Information Management and Systems*, Wagga Wagga: N.S.W. Centre for Information Studies, Charles Sturt University, 2000.

White I, Tacket A., "Exploring the Use of Narrative Analysis as an Operational Research Method: A Case Study in Voluntary Sector Evaluation", *Journal of the Operational Research Society*, 2000.

Yin R.K., *Case Study Research: Design and Methods*, 2nd ed. Newbury Park, Sage Publications, 1994.

10

Data Analysis and Interpretation of Results

Research carries vast applications for the persons working in the field of education by not only helping them enrich and contribute significantly to their field but also by helping them discharging their roles and duties effectively and efficiently. By conducting quality research they not only advance the knowledge but also serve for the cause of the welfare of the nation and humankind. In research, collecting genuine data carefully is very crucial, and analysing these data and interpreting the results are also equally significant. And, this process of research is incomplete without writing the research report.

10.1. Analysis of Data

In research, after formulating a problem, we collect raw data by administrating various types of educational tools (as per our research problem) on the selected sample. Then, we have to analyse and interpret these data to draw sound conclusions and valid generalisations. No matter how much valid, reliable and adequate the collected data may be these are useless if not processed carefully, means- carefully. This means that these need to be carefully organised, scientifically analysed, intelligently interpreted, and rationally generalised.

10.1.1. Qualitative Method of Data Analysis

As far as the nature of the data is concerned, it may be classified into two broad categories: "qualitative, and quantitative." The nature of the data largely depends on the type of the research tool or technique used by the researcher on the sample to collect these data. The data collected through open-ended questionnaires, participant observation, or an open-ended/unstructured interview are generally qualitative in nature which show what people uncover about themselves in their own words.

Many times, while doing research, information cannot be collected as scores but through words such information is called Qualitative Data. When you ask open-ended questions, e.g. you ask someone to explain his/her high school experiences, you get answers in words and statements which are known as qualitative because they express qualities rather than in the form of quantity.

The open-ended questionnaires, participant observation, and in-depth unstructured interviews provide us with qualitative data in bulks which are to be organised and classified into specific categories, patterns or descriptive units in order to avoid any confusion and chaos. Since there are no universal and formal rules to organise the data in these specific categories, the researcher has to adopt a creative approach to make the data systematic so that he/she may arrive at meaningful conclusions. But, first of all we should prepare at least four copies of the collected data, one of which should be stored in a safe place since these data are invaluable and unique. If something wrong happens to the original data, it is very much impossible to recollect the identical data no matter you may still have the same sample, same tools etc. Rest of the copies can be used to add comments in margins, and for cutting and pasting purposes in the process of converting the unorganised scattered data into organised and meaningful categories.

Analysis of the qualitative data means studying the organised material in order to discover inherent facts. These data are studied from as many angles as possible either to explore the new facts or to reinterpret already known existing facts. The mostly used analyses, in analysing the qualitative data, are content analysis, inductive analysis, and logical analysis.

10.1.2. Content Analysis

The nature of educational phenomena is not like that of physical phenomena. While the latter are largely quantitative and former are largely qualitative or abstract in nature, qualitative phenomena are vague and complex, and that's why clear results are not easily available in social sciences research. Content analysis' is a technique to achieve results from qualitative data collected through questionnaires, interviews or other methods. In content analysis, we reduce data into specific categories, scientific and objective facts. As per Berelson content analysis is a technique of social research which presents qualitative data in an objective, systematic and quantitative form. According to Kaplan, "Content analysis attempts to characterise the meaning in a given body to discourse in a systematic and quantitative fashion." So, it can be concluded that the main purpose of content analysis is to present the social phenomena in systematic, numerical and quantitative fashion. Following are the steps involved in the process of content analysis:

10.1.2.1 Defining the Units of Analysis

First of all, the researcher should define the material (unit) he/she wants to be analysed. The material may include single words, phrases, sentences, paragraphs, articles, or complete books. The selection of the unit totally depends on the research needs, and either of these serves as an entity whose specified characteristics the researcher wants to analyse.

10.1.2.2 Specifying Variables and Categories

The unit of study is also known as symbolic material, and the researcher tries to convert it into objective data. It is this objective data which is later put on scientific treatment and generalisation. To convert the symbolic material into objective data, we have to specify the 'variables' or dimensions or type of attributes in terms of which we later make descriptions.

10.1.2.3 Frequency, Direction and Intensity

After defining the unit to be studied, and specifying the variables along with their categories to be employed, we analyse the material in terms of frequency, direction and intensity. For frequency, the researcher just counts the number of units that fall into each of the specified categories. Direction refers to whether the reference studied was interesting/uninteresting, pleasant/unpleasant, favourable/unfavourable or neutral. Intensity specifies the emotional component in the units studied.

10.1.2.4. Sampling

It is of utmost importance that the analysed unit must be representative of the total material so that the results can be generalised accurately. Sampling is one of major and practical problems of content analysis.

10.1.2.5. Constructing the Content Analysis Outline

In order to avoid difficulties on a later stage, the researcher should clearly specify that which data are required in his/her research design. It also helps in planning the final tables which may be required later in content analysis.

For effective constructing of content analysis outline, the researcher should make explicit plans for the tabulation of the coded data. It should be planned in advance whether the data are to be tabulated manually (by hand) or to be punched on cards for machine processing (or for computer feeding).

The outline should be prepared very carefully and should contain sufficient details regarding the unit to be studied, the number of each enumeration unit, provisions for coding, the name of the coder and other relevant information, as the case may be. A researcher should use an exhaustive system with mutually exhaustive categories. The exhaustive system means that there is a category where we can place every relevant item found in content analysis. And, mutually exhaustive categories mean that an item must be placed on one and only one place within that system of categories. The researcher must prepare a manual of instructions with operational definitions of each and every category.

It is highly crucial that different coders must all unitise the same material in the same category. It is very essential for the scientific inference and objective generalisation of the findings. So the researcher must develop such a procedure for unitising the material.

Some pilot work on a sample of material should be done in order to determine whether some modifications are required in analysis outline and unitising procedure. After finalising the analysis outline and unitising procedure, the researcher should select different coders who can properly handle the data and use the analysis outline as properly as required. After selecting efficient coders, they should be given proper briefing and training so that they may fully understand the objectives and procedure of the research.

10.1.3. Inductive Analysis

Inductive analysis specifies that the themes, patterns and categories of analysis themselves emerge out of the data but it requires the researcher to look carefully for the variation in the data. In this regard, Patton says, "For evaluation, the study of natural variation will involve particular attention to variations in programme processes and how participants respond to and are affected by programmes. Two ways of representing the patterns emerge from analysis of data. First, the analyst can use the categories developed and articulated in the programme studied to organise presentation of particular themes. Second, the analyst may also become aware of categories or patterns for which the people in the programme did not have labels or terms, and the analyst develops terms to describe these inductively generated categories."

Patton names these approaches as indigenous and analyst-constructed typologies. In 'indigenous typologies', the researcher looks for the terms which emerge out of the group of people itself and studies and explains the group in the light of these terms. Whereas, in 'analyst-constructed typologies', when the researcher does not find already popular terms in the studied group, he has to construct the patterns, themes or categories on the bases of which he will further study the group.

10.1.4. Logical Analysis

Logical analysis aims at creating potential categories by crossing one typology with another, and then moving back and forth between the logical construction and the actual data for creating a "new typology" using cross-classification matrices. This kind of analysis requires the researcher to be extremely careful in creating such categories and sensitively and critically examining whether any particular behaviour has been overlooked in the data and whether he can logically set a category which has not been revealed before.

10.1.5. Quantitative Method of Data Analysis

Most of the times, the researchers want to obtain data in the form of scores because these can be very easily tabulated and analysed. Those measures which can be expressed in scores are known as quantitative data. As the name implies, these data show quantity. After the administration of various educational tools on selected sample, we get the quantitative data in raw forms. Then we need to organise, tabulate, analyse and interpret these data to draw sound conclusions and valid generalisations. "Raw score" simply means a numeral that is expressed by a test score or other direct measurement that has not been converted in any way.

The organisation of quantitative data includes editing, coding, classification and tabulation.

10.1.5.1. Editing

Editing is a process of examining the collected raw data (specially in surveys) to detect errors and omissions and to correct these when possible. As a matter of fact, editing involves a careful scrutiny of the completed questionnaires and/or schedules. Editing is done to assure that the data are accurate, consistent with other facts gathered, uniformly entered, as complete as possible and have been well arranged to facilitate coding and tabulation. This shows that editing is the first and very important step in the organisation of data.

10.1.5.2. Coding

Coding refers to the process of assigning numerals or other symbols to answers so that responses can be put into a limited number of categories or classes. Such classes should be appropriate to the research problem under consideration. They must also possess the characteristic of exhaustiveness (i.e. there must be a class for every data item) and also that of mutual exclusivity which means that a specific answer can be placed in one and only one cell in a given category set. Another rule to be observed is that of undimensionality by which is meant that every class is defined in terms of only one concept. In coding the data, rules of exhaustiveness, exclusiveness and undimensionality of the categories must be carefully followed.

10.1.5.3. Classification

Classification means dividing the raw data into different homogeneous categories, classes, groups, or heads on the basis of some common characteristics so that we may find some meaningful relationships. Two systems can be used in the classification of data. The first is to classify data on the basis of the descriptive characteristics of the sample (e.g., gender, literacy, etc.), and the second method is to classify data on the basis of numerals (e.g., age, income, height, weight, etc.).

10.1.5.4. Tabulation

When a mass of data has been assembled, it becomes necessary for the researcher to arrange the same in some kind of concise and logical order. This procedure is referred to as tabulation. Thus, tabulation is the process of summarising raw data and displaying the same in compact form (i.e., in the form of statistical tables) for further analysis. In a broader sense, tabulation is an orderly arrangement of data in columns and rows.

So, tabulation is an essential process that provides us with the basis for various statistical treatments of the tabulated data. Tabulation can be done both by hand or by mechanical or electronic devices.

10.1.6. Descriptive Method of Data Analysis

After using descriptive data analysis we can make generalisations about that particular group of individuals only whom we studied. We cannot extend our conclusions beyond that group. The data have described the characteristics of only this particular group, and provided desired information about the nature of that particular group only.

Statistical Measures: Several types of statistical measures are used in describing and analysing the data in a meaningful manner:

I. Measures of Central Tendency

   a) Mean

   b) Median

   c) Mode

II. Measures of Spread or Dispersion
   a) Range
   b) The Deviation from the Mean (x)
   c) Variance
   d) Standard Deviation

III. Measures of Relative Position
   a) Percentile Rank
   b) Percentile Score
   c) Standard Scores

IV. Measures of Relationship
   a) Coefficient of Correlation
   b) Pearson's Product-Moment Coefficient of Correlation
   c) Spearman Rank Order Coefficient of Correlation
   d) Phi Correlation Coefficient

10.1.7. Inferential Data Analysis

The ultimate purpose of research is to discover general principles based upon the observed relationship between variables. The research process would have become never-ending and prohibitively expensive if we had to observe the whole population. Inferential data analysis is the practical solution. In this type of analysis the sampling process is always involved and we study a small group that is assumed to be representative of that population from which it was drawn. This small group is called "sample" and the large group from which the sample is selected is known as "population".

Statistical Measures: Following statistical measures are very common in use for analysing the data:

I. Parametric Tests:
   a) t-test
   b) ANOVA (analysis of variance)
   c) ANCOVA (analysis of co-variance)
   d) Factor analysis
   e) Pearson's r

II. Nonparametric Tests:
   a) The Chi Square test
   b) The Mann-Whitney test
   c) Wilcoxon test
   d) Spearman's rho

10.2. Interpretation of Results

Data can be classified as qualitative and quantitative, these are to be interpreted distinctively.

10.2.1. Interpretation of Qualitative Data

Interpretation involves explaining the findings, answering "why" questions, attaching significance to particular results, and putting patterns into an analytic framework. It is tempting to rush into the creative work of interpreting the data before doing the detailed, hard work of putting together coherent answers to major descriptive questions. But description comes first. The discipline and rigor of qualitative analysis depend on presenting solid descriptive data.

As far as the interpretation of the qualitative data is concerned, it is more dependent on the researchers' research skills, research background, intelligence, creativity, and biases. It is most difficult to objectively interpret qualitative data than the quantitative data because the latter are derived directly from the numerical analysis of the data. This descriptive knowledge, on the basis of which the interpreter interprets his/her findings, is essential not only for the interpreter but also for the reader so that he/she may fully understand that how the interpreter has reached on this conclusion.

10.2.2. Interpretation of Quantitative Data

After collecting and analysing the quantitative data, the researcher can now move to the final stage of interpreting the results. The data don't speak and interpret themselves rather it is the researcher who provides tongue and words to the data, and give a meaning to the data in light of his research problem. Interpretation requires very careful efforts on the part of the researcher so that he/she may well recognise and accept his/her own biases and subjectivity, and must be able to control these in order to give due place to objectivity while interpreting the results.

10.2.3. Characteristics of Good Interpretation

10.2.3.1. Free from Subjectivity

The interpreter must be able to check his/her own biases and subjectivity while interpreting the results and he must objectively interpret his/her result findings.

10.2.3.2. To-the-Point Interpretation

Only that interpretation can be regarded as good that is to the point, no important point is left and no irrelevant point is stressed.

10.2.3.3. Apt Findings/Views

A careless and inadequate expression of the findings will lead to nothing but confusion, disinterest and harm to knowledge. So, the results must be interpreted and expressed clearly.

10.2.3.4. Resort in Entire Knowledge

While interpreting his/her findings, the researcher must stress how his/her results support or differ with the old research studies done in the similar area.

10.2.3.5. Ready to Face Shortcomings

A good interpreter, instead of hiding his/her shortcomings which had influenced his/her research work, accept and clearly explain them so that the future researchers may take care of these.

10.2.3.6. Simple and Clear Language

A good interpretation is that one which is in simple and influential language. The interpreters must avoid using the flowery language while interpreting their results.

10.2.3.7. Giving Suggestions for Future Research

A researcher, while doing his/her study becomes deeply involved in it and gets many new ideas. He/she should try to give enough space in his/her report to these new ideas for future researches.

10.2.4. Foundations of the Interpretation of Results

The interpretation of results should be based on:

10.2.4.1. Research Problem

An interpretation should be to the point and the findings must be interpreted in the light of the problems formulated by the researcher to study.

10.2.4.2.Hypotheses

Hypotheses are the tentative solutions to the research problems and are formulated before the data are gathered. Interpretations should reveal whether these hypotheses were rejected or retained.

10.2.4.3. Statistical Analyses and Findings

Various types of statistical procedures can be used as per the research needs of the researcher and interpretation should be based on these that which statistical test revealed what types of the results.

10.2.4.4. Observations

Sometimes during conducting a research study, the researcher might see some unhypothesised relationships between variables that should not be ignored and should be given due recognition. These may serve as the basis for future research.

10.2.5. Precautions in Results Interpretion

Just a little carelessness at this final stage of interpretation can result in the misinterpretation of the results that not only cause harm to the knowledge but also misguide future research projects based on these misinterpretations. This will also result in the wastage of money, time, energy and resources on a large scale with an end result of a big zero. Thus, it is also a highly precious step in research as are the previous ones. So, it is crucial to identify and check the possible errors that can be made in the interpretation of the results. The following are some common errors of interpretation that we must take care of and avoid:

10.2.5.1. Failure to See the Problem in Proper Perspective

Many times the researchers don't have a clear idea of their problem because it was in a majority of cases assigned to them by their research guide. Instead of perceiving their problem in a broad sense with a clear, global perspective they just focus on its present, immediate impact. So, they should have a clear vision with proper orientation in their problems for the long term benefits.

10.2.5.2. Failure to Appreciate the Relevance of Various Elements

Many times research studies (pseudoresearches) are undertaken just for the sake of prestige or status associated with these, and mostly investigators even cannot explain the operational definitions of their chief variables they have studied. They also have a very poor orientation in the relevance of various other variables that might be associated with or influence their study. So, a good researcher should give due importance to various relevant elements in interpreting their findings.

10.2.5.3. Failure to Recognise Limitations in the Research Evidence

No research is free from limitations which may be of any type like non-representativeness of the sample, inadequate research design, use of improper tools and inappropriate statistical analysis. The interpreter should be able to recognise his limitations, if any, and interpret his findings in light of these limitations.

10.2.5.4. Misinterpretation Due to Unstudied Factors

The obtained findings are not just a result of any single factor rather there may be many latent unrecognised factors that might have influenced the findings. A researcher should extensively study the literature and present a clear broad picture of his field of interest.

10.2.5.5. Ignoring Selective Factors

A researcher may misinterpret his/her findings if he/she ignores the selective factors. It becomes clear from the studies in which the researcher selects a particular group to study or where a significant factor is playing major role in the situation studied.

10.2.5.6. Difficulties of Interpretative Evaluation

In descriptive research, one cannot properly interpret the data unless one does not properly evaluate the facts. The researcher will have to study and evaluate the curriculum him/herself and assume that his/her interpretation is correct in the light of the gathered facts.

10.2.5.7. Interpreting Expected Findings

Even if we get the expected results, while interpreting these we should not go beyond the supporting data, and we should not forget and ignore the limitations of our study. Even we should check our inborn and unconscious tendency to report expected findings.

10.2.5.8. Interpreting Unexpected Findings or Negative Results

It creates a lot of tension if we get unexpected or negative results than what we had thought of or hypothesised. It should be always remembered that these hypotheses are just the tentative solutions to the problems based on the guesswork and are not the real solutions. Results may or may not confirm hypotheses. Then, we should, reconsider the original hypotheses in the light of the present findings, and interpret our results. We should not be reluctant in reporting contradictory findings because this is not a fair attitude and it blocks the progress of research and knowledge. And above all, if you get negative results also than what you had expected, these are also significant findings and you must report these as these are with full confidence in you and your methodology.

10.3. Conclusion

Analysis of data and its interpretations pocess a very important place in the research process. A number of statistical methods also assist the researcher to interpret the results. A good analysis leads to good interpretation and it ultimately leads to a goods research. So, be careful to keep off from wrong interpretations.

References

Miles, B. M., & Huberman, A. M., *Qualitative data analysis: A sourcebook of new methods*, Beverly Hills, CA: Sage Publications, Inc., 1984.

Morse, J. M., *Critical issues in qualitative research methods*, Thousand Oaks, CA: Sage Publications, 1993.

Moustakas, P. H., *Phenomenological research methods*, Thousand Oaks, CA: Sage Publications, 1994.

Sapsford, R & Jupp, V. (Eds.), *Data collection and analysis*, Thousand Oaks, CA: Sage, 1996.

Yin, R. K., *Case study research: Design and methods*, Thousand Oaks, CA: Sage Publications, 1994.

11

Preparing the Research Report

A research paper is a piece of writing that reports facts, data, and other information on a specific topic. It's called a research paper because you research your subject before writing your paper. Even a good quality research is of no use unless the findings are made known to other people. Writing research reports can do this.

11.1. Purposes of Report Writing

11.1.1. To Express Findings

After conducting some research work we wish to express our findings and views. Writing reports is a very effective communication medium by the help of which we can effectively express our research findings and views.

11.1.2. To Share the Findings

When we conduct some research we certainly get results which may be of some interest to people of the concerned field. It would be impossible for us to repeat our findings verbally again and again if somebody comes and asks about these. To share our findings, we have to get these written and published so that interested people can approach these wherever they are, read these and get advantage of these findings.

11.1.3. To Spread Knowledge

That research, no matter how noble or golden it is, is of no use which is just restricted to the briefcase of its investigator or which does not cross the threshold of its lab. Every research is done to advance and spread the knowledge and this will become impossible without report writing.

11.1.4. For Benefiting Others

The practical utility of writing down a research work is that other people without repeating the same research get acquainted with more and more phenomena and get advantage of this knowledge.

11.1.5. To get Scientific Approval

Unless the research report is written and got published, it cannot be put to scientific verification. It is after this verification that the true relationship between different phenomena can be established.

11.1.6. For Future Reference

The researcher, while conducting his/her research, experiences a lot of different and unique ideas that may generate and invite some crucial research in future too. And, the world would remain unaware of these unique ideas if the researcher keeps these precious ideas buried.

Although different institutions or universities have established their unique styles of writing theses or dissertations, yet all agree with its purpose of correct, easy and conformed presentation. Research reports should be clear, organised and properly presented in an order to communicate the ideas effectively. Research reports, being relatively concise, differ somewhat from the thesis or dissertation.

11.2. Components of a Research Report

The common components of a research report submitted for a degree requirement, consist of preliminary pages, the main body of the report, and the appendixes.

11.2.1. Preliminary Pages

Title page—The title page usually includes the title of the report, the author's name, the degree requirement being fulfilled, the name and location of the college or university awarding the degree, the date of submission of the the report, and signatures of approving committee members. The title should describe the purpose of the study as clearly as possible.

Acknowledgements page—The acknowledgements page allows the writer to express appreciation to persons who have contributed significantly to the completion of the report.

Table of contents—The table of contents is basically an outline of your report that indicates on which page each main section (or chapter) and subsection begins.

List of Tables and figures—The list of tables and figures, which is presented on a separate page, gives the number and title of each table and figure and the page on which it can be found.

Abstract—Most colleges and universities require an abstract or summary of the study. The number of pages for each will be specified; they usually range from 100 to 500 words. The abstract should describe the most important aspects of the study, including the problem investigated, the type of participants and instruments, the design, the procedures, the major results, and the major conclusions.

11.2.2. Main Body of the Report

Introduction—The introduction section is the first section of the main body of the report and includes a well-written description of the problem, a review of related literature, a statement of the hypothesis, and definition of terms. The introduction also includes operational definitions of terms used in the study that do not have a commonly known meaning.

11.2.3. Statement of the Problem

Review of Related Literature—The review of related literature describes and analyses what has already been done related to your problem.

Statement of the Hypothesis—A good hypothesis in a quantitative study states as clearly and concisely as possible the expected relationship (or difference) between two variables, and defines those variables in operational, measurable terms.

11.3. Patterns of Research Report

11.3.1. Title Page

It is the very first page of the research report and includes only the title, author's name and affiliation separated by double space. Title should be concise and a perfect indicator of the purpose of the study typed in upper and lower cases, centered and double spaced if it is in two lines. The author's affiliation appears just beneath his/her name and near the top of the page. Acknowledgements indicate the basis of the study (e.g., doctoral research), grant support, and assistance in doing this research, etc.; and should be typed in single space, followed by the running head separated by double space. The running head is a shortened version of the title and is typed in uppercase letters near the bottom of the page.

11.3.2. Abstract

It appears on the second page of the research report, describes the research, includes the summary of problems studied, characteristics of the sample, tools used, research findings, and the conclusions drawn by the researcher.

11.3.3. Body

The main organs of the body of research report are introduction, method, results and discussion.

11.3.4. Introduction

It starts on the third page without a label of "Introduction," and includes the following: (i) the statement of the problem which must be clear, concise and definite, (ii) review of pertinent literature that is highly related to the researched problem only, and (iii) hypotheses which should be justified by giving clear rationale, operational definitions of the variables to be studied, and proper and formal statements of various hypotheses.

11.3.5. Method

It follows the 'introduction'. In it, the researcher explains intelligently what and how he/she did to conduct the research. It should be written very carefully so that future researchers may replicate the study if required. This section begins with a centered head "Method" and its subheadings are placed at the left side and are underlined. The subsection on 'subjects' explains the sample characteristics, e.g., number of subjects studied, procedure of sample selection, their demographic characteristics, such as age groups, gender, caste, socioeconomic status etc. as per the requirement of the study. Very precise information about the 'tools' used should be given in sufficient details (such as the author, tool description, reliability and validity, etc) so that the future researchers may get a clear idea if they want to replicate the study. 'Procedure' describes those steps in past tense which were actually carried out by the researcher in conducting the research. It should be written very carefully and minutely. No relevant information should be left unreported.

11.3.6. Results

It carefully (and in proper organisation) presents the data, the statistical analyses applied on the data, and the results. It is not concerned with the discussion of the implications of the findings. This section presents all the relevant findings, whether supporting the hypotheses or not. Tables and figures are used to supplement the textual presentation. Complete statistical calculations and formulas are avoided in the research reports except the unusual ones, and the level of significance for statistical analyses are reported very carefully, with the help of tables.

11.3.7. Discussion

It is the final organ of the body of a research report. After the careful presentation of the results, one can move to determine the theoretical as well as practical implications of the study, focusing on whether the solutions to the original problems are approached, hypotheses are supported or rejected as the case may be. Suggestions for future research should be incorporated here.

11.3.8. References

References' section begins on a new page with the heading in center. It specifies all those documents, books, journals etc, which are mentioned by the researcher in his/her report. References are given in an alphabetical order and each one starts at the left margin of the page, with the rest of the lines double spaced. References are given in the text by giving the last name of the author and the year of publication in parentheses that are separated by a comma. Varieties of referencing styles are there;

only one thing is to be remembered: that in all references follow one consistent style all through.

An 'appendix' (plural appendices) provides detailed information which could not be placed in the main body of the report. Like references, each appendix starts on a new page and its heading is also centered. Writing an effective research report is not an easy task, and even experienced researchers do it with excessive care and patience, and revise many times before the submission. We must take care of and avoid spelling errors, inconsistent tense sequence. Generally, many mistakes are done in reporting the references.

11.4. Conclusion

Report writing is the final stage of a research journey. Here reveals a researcher's dalliance with words. A research report should be handled dexterously. Research is a process, which should be conducted dedication and it demands hard work. Whatever may be the predicament a researcher suffers while conducting a research, a badly written report will make all these hardships meaningless. So, a research should be written with simple words and should be readable. She/he must give full concentration for making a research meaningful.

References

Best, J. W. and Kahn, J. V., *Research in Education*, New Delhi: Prentice-Hall of India Pvt. Ltd., 1992.

Best, J. W., "An analysis of certain selected factors underlying the choice of teaching as a profession", 1948.

Koul, L., *Methodology of Educational Research*, New Delhi: Vikas Publishing House Pvt. Ltd., 1997.

Rosander, A. C., "The Spearman - Brown formula in attitude scale construction", *Journal of Experimental Psychology*, 1936.

12

Validity and Accuracy of Research

Validity is an element of educational research which addresses the issues of whether the researcher is actually measuring what s/he says s/he is. As an example, let us pretend we want to measure attitude. A psychologist by the name of Kurt Goldstein developed a way to measure "abstract attitude" by assessing several different abilities in brain injury patients, such as ability to separate their internal experience from the external world, ability to shift from one task to another, and the ability to recognise an organised whole, to break it into component parts, and then reorganise it as before. Carl Jung defined attitude a introversion and extraversion. Raymond Cattell defined attitude in three components: intensity of interest, interest in an action, and interest in action toward an object.

Validity in educational research has several different components—some people feel there are only three components of validity , and others feel there are four components of validity. All of these facets of validity you would ideally want to establish for your research measure prior to administering it for your actual research project.

12.1. Face Validity

It requires that your measure appears relevant to your construct to an innocent bystander, or more specifically, to those you wish to measure. Face validity can be established by your Mom—just ask her if she thinks your survey could adequately and completely assess someone's attitude. If Mom says yes, then you have face validity. However, you may want to take this one step further and ask individuals similar to those you wish to study if they feel the same way your Mom does about your survey. The reason for asking these people is that people can sometimes become resentful and uncooperative if they think they are being misrepresented to others, or worse, if they think you are misrepresenting yourself to them.

In order to have a valid measure of a social construct, one should never stop at achieving only face validity, as this is not sufficient. However one should never skip establishing face validity, because if you do not have it, you cannot achieve the other components of validity.

12.2. Content Validity

Content validity is very similar to face validity, except instead of asking your Mom or your target members of your population of interest, you must ask experts in the field. The theory behind content validity, as opposed to face validity, is that experts are aware of nuances in the construct that may be rare or elusive of which the layperson may not be aware. Many studies proceed following content validity achievement, however this does not necessarily mean the measures used are entirely valid.

12.2.1. Criterion Validity

Criterion validity is a more rigorous test than face or content validity. Criterion validity means your attitude assessment can predict or agree with constructs external to attitude. Two types of criterion validity exist:

— *Predictive validity*: If you administer your attitude survey to someone and s/he rates high, indicating a positive attitude, then alter that week s/he is fired from his/her job and his/her spouse divorces him/her, you may not have predictive validity.

— *Concurrent validity*: If you administer your attitude survey to someone who is cheerful and smiling a lot, but they rate low, indicating a negative attitude, your survey may not have concurrent validity.

12.2.2. Construct Validity

Finally, the most rigorous validity test you can put your attitude survey through is the construct validity check. If your attitude survey has construct validity, lower attitude scores (indicating negative attitude) should correlate negatively with life satisfaction survey scores, nd positively with life stress scores. These other constructs do not necessarily have to be predictive or concurrent, however often times they are.

12.3. Drawbacks of Validity Test

Researchers who have evaluated experimental research have described a number of factors that can limit the validity of a research study. The validity of a study is related to the design of the experiment and the research can modify the effects of these factors on the research by selecting a research design that guards against the threats to validity. The threats to experimental validity can be classified into two:

i) Threats to internal validity,
ii) Threats to external validity.

A study is internally valid when the results or effects on the dependent variable are attributable to the independent variable and not to other factors. How well these other factors are controlled is related to the internal validity of the study.

External validity, sometimes called ecological validity, is concerned with the generalisability of the study. The degree to which the results of the study can be generalized to groups beyond the study sample is an indication of the external validity of the study.

12.3.1. Threats to Internal Validity

i) *History*—Unexpected events occur between the pre- and posttest, affecting the dependent variable.
ii) *Maturation*—Changes occur in the participants, from growing older, wiser, more experienced, etc. during the study.
iii) *Testing*—Taking a pretest alters the result of the posttest.
iv) *Instrumentation*—The measuring instrument is changed between pre- and post testing or a single measuring instrument is unreliable.
v) *Statistical Regression*—Extremely high or extremely low scorers tend to regress to the mean on retesting.

vi) *Differential Selection of Participants*—Participants in the experimental and control groups have different characteristics that affect the dependent variable differently.

vii) *Mortality*—Different participants drop out of the study in different numbers, altering the composition of the treatment groups.

viii) *Selection-Maturation Interaction*—The participants selected into treatment groups have different maturation rates. Selection interactions also occur with history and instrumentation.

12.3.2 Threats to External Validity

i) Pretest-Treatment Interaction—The pretest sensitises participants to aspects of the treatment and thus influences posttest scores.

ii) Selection-Treatment Interaction—The nonrandom or volunteer selection of participants limits the generalisability of the study.

iii) Multiple Treatment Interference—When participants receive more than one treatment, the effect of prior treatment can affect or interact with later treatments, limiting generalisability.

iv) Specificity of Variables—Poorly operationalised variables make it difficult to identify the setting and procedures to which the variables can be generalised.

v) Treatment Diffusion—Treatment groups communicate and adopt pieces of each other's treatment, altering the initial status of the treatments comparison.

vi) Experimenter Effects—Conscious or unconscious actions of the researcher affects participants' performance and responses.

12.4. Accuracy

Some common worries amongst researchers are:

— Will the research I've done stand up to outside scrutiny?

— Will anyone believe my findings?

These questions are addressed by researchers by assessing the data collection method (the research instrument) for its reliability and its validity.

12.4.1. Reliability

Reliability is the extent to which the same finding will be obtained if the research was repeated at another time by another researcher. If the same finding can be obtained again, the instrument is consistent or reliable.

12.4.2. Validity

Validity is epitomised by the question: 'Are we measuring what we think we are measuring?' This is very difficult to assess. The following questions are typical of those asked to assess validity issues:

- — Has the researcher gained full access to the knowledge and meanings of informants?
- — Would experienced researchers use the same questions or methods?

No procedure is perfectly reliable, but if a data collection procedure is unreliable then it is also invalid, but if it is reliable then it is not necessarily valid.

12.4.3. Triangulation

Triangulation is crosschecking of data using multiple data sources or using two or more methods of data collection. There are different types of triangulation, including:

- — Time triangulation—longitudinal studies
- — Methodological triangulation—same method at different times or different methods on same object of study
- — Investigator triangulation—uses more than one researcher.

12.4.4. Sampling Error

Sampling error is a measure of the difference between the sample results and the population parameters being measured. It can never be eliminated, but if random sampling is used, sampling error occurs by chance but is reduced as the sample size increases. When non-random sampling is used this is not the case.

12.4..5. Non-sampling Error

All errors, other than sampling errors, are non-sampling errors and can never be eliminated. The many sources of non-sampling errors include the following:

- Researcher error—unclear definitions; reliability and validity issues; data analysis problems, for example, missing data.
- Interviewer error—general approach; personal interview techniques; recording responses.
- Respondent error—inability to answer; unwilling; cheating; not available; low response rate.

12.5. Conclusion

The importance and usefulness of a research is determined by its validity. A research is valid when it has fewer errors. Research is prone to errors at any of its stage. Mostly errors happen while the collection of data and its interpretation. Data should be accurate and its interpretation must be correct. Only then a researcher can produce a valid research. A researcher must be careful in each and every stages of research. Checking and counter checking will help to tackle errors. A valid research will be worthwhile for generation after generation.

References

Brinberg, D. & McGrath, J.E., *Validity and the research process*, Beverly Hills: Sage Publications, 1985.

Carmines, E. G. & Zeller, R.A., *Reliability and validity assessment*, Newbury Park: Sage Publications, 1991.

Fink, A., ed., *How to measure survey reliability and validity*, Thousand Oaks, CA: Sage, 1995.

Kirk, J. & Miller, M. M., *Reliability and validity in qualitative research*, Beverly Hills: Sage Publications, 1986.

Merriam, S. B., "What can you tell from an N of 1?: Issues of validity and reliability in qualitative research", *Journal of Lifelong Learning*, 1995.

Bibliography

Berg, B.L., *Qualitative Research Methods for the Social Science*, Allyn and Bacon, 1989.

Best, J. W. and Kahn, J. V., *Research in Education*, New Delhi: Prentice-Hall of India Pvt. Ltd., 1992.

Best, J. W., "An analysis of certain selected factors underlying the choice of teaching as a profession", 1948.

Best, John W., *Research in Education*, Englewood Cliffs, New Jersey: Prantice Hall Inc., 1977.

Borg, W.R., and Gall, M.D., *Educational Research: An Introduction*, (Fifth edition) Longman, 1989.

Boruch, R.F., "Coupling randomized experiments and approximations to experiments in social program evaluation", *Sociological Methods and Research*, 1975.

Brinberg, D. & McGrath, J.E., *Validity and the research process*, Beverly Hills: Sage Publications, 1985.

Buch, M. B., *A Survey of Research in Education*, Baroda: CASE, M. S. University, Baroda, 1974.

Bulmer, M., *Sociological Research Methods*, (Second edition) Macmillan, 1984.

Campbell, A., *Practitioner research and professional development in Education*, London: Paul Chapman, 2004.

Campbell, D. T. and Stanley, J. C., "Experimental and quasi-experimental designs for research on teaching", In N. L. Gage (Ed.) *Handbook of Research in Teaching*, Chicago: Rand McNally and Company, 1963.

_______________ ., *Experimental and Quasi-Experimental Designs for Research*, Rand McNally, Chicago, Illinois, 1963, 1966.

Carmines, E. G. & Zeller, R.A., *Reliability and validity assessment*, Newbury Park: Sage Publications, 1991.

Chandra, S. S. and Sharma, R. K., *Research in Education*, New Delhi: Atlantic Publishers and Distributors, 1997.

Christensen, L. B., *Experimental Methodology* (6th ed.), Boston: Allyn and Bacon, 1994.

Cohen, L., and Manion, I., *Research Methods in Education*, Routledge, 1989.

Cook, T.D. and Campbell, D.T., *Quasi-Experimentation: Design and Analysis for Field Settings*, Rand McNally, Chicago, Illinois, 1979.

Corey, S. M., *Action Research to Improve School Practices*, New York: Teachers College, Columbia University, 1953.

Cross, N (ed.), *Developments in Design Methodology*, Chichester, UK: John Wiley & Sons Ltd., 1984.

Dadds, M. and Hart, S. (Eds), *Doing Practitioner Research Differently*, Routledge Falmer, 2001.

Dey, I., *Qualitative data analysis: A user-friendly guide for social scientists*, New York: Routledge, 1993.

Dominowski, R.L., *Research Methods*, Prentice-Hall, 1980.

Ely, M., Anzul, M., Friedman, T., Garner, D., and Steinmetz, A.M., *Doing Qualitative Research: Circles within Circles*, Falmer Press, 1990.

Falmer Press McNeill, P., *Research Methods*, (Second edition) Routledge, 1990.

Fink, A., ed., *How to measure survey reliability and validity*, Thousand Oaks, CA: Sage, 1995.

Freeman, *Doing Teacher –Research: From Inquiry to Understanding*, Boston, Heinle and Heinle, 1998.

Gillespie, M., "Research Within Reach", *Focus on Basics 2*, Spring, 1989.

Goetz, J. and LeCompte, M., *Ethnography and Qualitative Design in Educational Research*, London: Academic Press, 1984.

Golden-Biddle, K and Locke, K., *Composing Qualitative Research*, Sage: Thousand Oaks, 1997.

Good, C. V., Barr, A. S., and Scates, D. E., *Methodology of Educational Research*, New York: Appleton-Century Crofts, Inc., 1941.

Gordon Wells (Editor), *Action, Talk, and Text: Learning and Teaching Through Inquiry*, Practitioner InquiryTeachers College Press, 2000.

Hammersley, M., *Educational Research: Policymaking and Practice*, London, Paul Chapman Publishing, 2002.

Isaac, S., and Michael, W.B., *Handbook in Research and Evaluation for Education and the Behavioural Sciences*, EdITS Publishers, 1989.

Judd, C.M. and Kenny, D.A., *Estimating the Effects of Social Interventions*, Cambridge University Press, Cambridge, MA., 1981.

Kelle, U. (Ed.), *Computer-aided qualitative data analysis,* Thousand Oaks, CA: SAGE, 1995.

Kerlinger, F. N., *Foundations of Behavioural Research* (2nd ed.), Delhi: Surjeet Publications, 1983.

Kirchhoff, K. T., "Design of questionnaires and structured interviews", In M. A. Mateo & K. T. Kirchhoff (Eds.), *Using and conducting nursing research in the clinical setting,* Philadelphia: Saunders, 1999.

Kirk, J. & Miller, M. M., *Reliability and validity in qualitative research,* Beverly Hills: Sage Publications, 1986.

Knafl, K.A., & Webster, D.C., "Managing and analyzing qualitative data: A description of tasks, techniques, and materials", *Western Journal of Nursing Research,* 1988.

Kothari, C. R., *Research Methodology: Methods and Techniques* (2nd ed.), New Delhi: Wishwa Prakashan, 1990.

Koul, Lokesh, *Methodology of Educational Research,* New Delhi: Vikas Publishing House Pvt. Ltd., 1984.

Laurel, B., *Design Research: Methods and Perspectives,* Cambridge: M.I.T. Press, 2003.

Marx, M. H., *Theories in Contemporary Psychology,* New York: Macmillan, 1963.

Maxwell, J. A., "Understanding and validity in qualitative research", *Harvard Educational Review,* 1992.

May, K.A., "Interview techniques in qualitative research: Concerns and challenges", In J.M. Morse (Ed.), *Qualitative nursing research: A contemporary dialogue,* Newbury Park, CA: Sage, 1991.

Merriam, S. B., "What can you tell from an N of 1?: Issues of validity and reliability in qualitative research", *Journal of Lifelong Learning,* 1995.

Middlewood, David, Coleman, M. and Lumby, J., *Practitioner Research in Education: Making a Difference,* Paul Chapman, 1999.

Miles, B. M., & Huberman, A. M., *Qualitative data analysis: A sourcebook of new methods,* Beverly Hills, CA: Sage Publications, Inc., 1984.

Monroe, Walters S. ed. *Encyclopaedia of Educational Research,* New York: The MacMillan Company, 1950.

Morse, J. M., *Critical issues in qualitative research methods,* Thousand Oaks, CA: Sage Publications, 1993.

_______________ ., "Emerging from the data": The cognitive processes of analysis in qualitative inquiry, In J. M. Morse (Ed.), *Critical issues in qualitative research methods,* Thousand Oaks, CA: Sage, 1994.

Moustakas, P. H., *Phenomenological research methods,* Thousand Oaks, CA: Sage Publications, 1994.

Nachmias, D. and Nachmias, C., *Research Methods in the Social Sciences,* New York: St. Martin's Press, 1981.

Newman I., *Qualitative-Quantitative Research Methodology: Exploring the Interactive Continuum,* Carbondale: Southern Illinois University Press, 1998.

Rosander, A. C., "The Spearman - Brown formula in attitude scale construction", *Journal of Experimental Psychology,* 1936.

Rowley, J. and Slack, F., "Conducting a Literature Review", *Management Research News,* 2004.

Sapsford, R & Jupp, V. (Eds.), *Data collection and analysis,* Thousand Oaks, CA: Sage, 1996.

Travers, Robert M. W., *An Introduction to Educational Research,* New York: The MacMillan Company, 1958.

Wallace, M. J., *Action Research for Language Teachers,* Cambridge: Cambridge University Press, 1998.

White I, Tacket A., "Exploring the Use of Narrative Analysis as an Operational Research Method: A Case Study in Voluntary Sector Evaluation", *Journal of the Operational Research Society,* 2000.

Williamson K., *Research Methods for Students and Professionals: Information Management and Systems,* Wagga Wagga: N.S.W. Centre for Information Studies, Charles Sturt University, 2000.

Yin R.K., *Case Study Research: Design and Methods,* 2nd ed. Newbury Park, Sage Publications, 1994.

Index